"Finally, a book about the kind of heartbreak that is so often dismissed or never even talked about. Christina takes the reader by the hand through this world of silent losses and helps them understand not only why they have been anxiously stuck in the past but how to find their way back to themselves."

Leeza Gibbons
New York Times bestselling author and founder of Leeza's Care Connection

"I think we're surprised by how the 'invisible' can sometimes have the greatest impact on our lives. I'm thankful to Christina for lifting us all up by helping us bring the invisible to life and understand how we can all find our place as 'watcher and thriver with a sprinkle of survivor'—a wonderful analog to crewmates having successful missions on a spaceship. By behaving like crewmates, not passengers, we have the power to create a future for ourselves and for all life on Earth that's as beautiful as it looks from space."

Astronaut Nicole Stott
author of *Back to Earth*

"If you feel stuck in the waiting room of a half-lived, wounded life, this book presents a strategy of self-discovery that takes you from surviving to thriving: out of the prison of your comfort zone and into the arms of the world."

Justine Musk

"Suffering is inevitable, and yet no one gives us a guide on how to deal with and heal our wounds. *Invisible Loss* is that manual. It shows how to turn pain into purpose, suffering into a source of meaning, and hurt into a way to help."

Dr. Jade Teta
author of *Human 365*

"Every journey needs a map, or guidebook, to help us on our way. Christina has poignantly and sensitively created just such a road map for everyone that struggles into a life reentry. A book for everyone to read. Simply awesome."

Ray Zahab
adventurer and author of *Running for My Life*

"In her latest book, Christina Rasmussen undertakes a courageous exploration of a subject within the complexity of loss that is often overlooked and deeply misunderstood. *Invisible Loss* delves into the nuanced terrain of personal transformation and the subtle yet profound shifts within our lives as we experience the many losses presented on our journey. Regardless of the catalyst to loss, we all face moments of impact that shift our world. With eloquence and keen insight, Christina examines the subconscious minefield that is experienced universally but often is not recognized or seen. This book serves as not only an important validation for our unseen pain but also a step-by-step guide to shifting from the waiting room, the awareness of one's self, and reentry into what comes next. In each chapter, the author invites you to sit with her for coffee breaks and do the hard but necessary work to reenter life not only on your terms but in a way that will reveal the hidden parts previously left behind—a must-read for anyone ready to move forward to find their inner thriver."

Michelle Steinke-Baumgard
author of *Healthy Healing*

"A profoundly important book for anyone who is dealing with grief. Christina has walked the talk, and her insight and wisdom is apparent on every page."

Jane Green
New York Times bestselling author and Dear Jane Advice Columnist

Invisible Loss

Also by Christina Rasmussen

Second Firsts: A Step-by-Step Guide to Life After Loss

*Where Did You Go? A Life-Changing Journey
to Connect with Those We've Lost*

Invisible Loss

Recognizing and Healing the
Unacknowledged Heartbreak
of Everyday Grief

Christina Rasmussen

sounds true
BOULDER, COLORADO

Sounds True
Boulder, CO

This book is not intended as a substitute for the medical recommendations of
physicians, mental health professionals, or other health-care providers. Rather, it is
intended to offer information to help the reader cooperate with physicians, mental
health professionals, and health-care providers in a mutual quest for optimal well-
being. We advise readers to carefully review and understand the ideas presented and
to seek the advice of a qualified professional before attempting to use them.

All names used throughout the book have been changed to protect patients' privacy.

Published 2024

Cover design by Jennifer Miles
Book design by Charli Barnes

Printed in the United States of America

BK06546

Library of Congress Cataloging-in-Publication Data

Names: Rasmussen, Christina, 1972- author.
Title: Invisible loss: recognizing and healing the unacknowledged heartbreak of every-
day grief/ Christina Rasmussen.
Description: Boulder, CO : Sounds True, 2024. | Includes bibliographical references.
Identifiers: LCCN 2023034909 (print) | LCCN 2023034910 (ebook) |
   ISBN 9781649630070 (trade paperback) | ISBN 9781649630087 (ebook)
Subjects: LCSH: Grief. | Loss (Psychology) | Change (Psychology).
Classification: LCC BF575.G7 R37 2024 (print) | LCC BF575.G7 (ebook) |
   DDC 155.9/3--dc23/eng/20230919
LC record available at https://lccn.loc.gov/2023034909
LC ebook record available at https://lccn.loc.gov/2023034910

To my daughters, Elina and Isabel, the gifts of my life

Contents

Introduction

M any people carry around a feeling of sadness that is difficult to share or even attempt to articulate clearly. This feeling is not easy to detect, especially if nothing particularly tragic or trying has taken place in the recent weeks or months of our lives. How you seem from the outside may not point to any reason for grief, as you may appear just fine to most, including yourself. But deep down, you could be carrying a type of burden that is almost like deadweight; it is heavy but subtle. You may not be sure if there is truly something to worry about, as some days feel easier than others and you have yet to acknowledge this heaviness even to yourself. When you feel this burden, you might ignore it; yet you notice other changes within you, discreet at first, until the feeling starts impacting your day-to-day routine.

How this subtle burden impacts you is intriguing, as you may simply find yourself moving some of your work meetings to the following week without recognizing the correlation between feeling off and rescheduling your calendar, or you may get invited to a dinner party and dread it. Nevertheless, you show up with a bottle of wine and a big smile on your face, as if nothing is wrong. You've swallowed these vague feelings of anxiety and sometimes nervousness for a while; after all, you have been taught to count your blessings. When you find yourself having an off day, you worry that you will be seen as a complainer, so you persevere. Except this angst you are carrying, an unsettled feeling first thing in the morning or the certain kind of tiredness that greets you in midafternoon, comes from grief. But not the kind of grief we think we know about or a type of loss we are accustomed to. Most people, believe it or not, won't know when this loss initially took place or how they've changed because of it.

Let me explain.

Most of us think of grief in terms of the way we feel when tragedy strikes, like the loss of a loved one or a devastating divorce. The label *grief* can also be applied to other somber times, such as when a beloved pet dies or when we move and have to say goodbye to our friends. What I mean here, though, is something else: the unacknowledged form of grief that arises when we feel overlooked, misunderstood, or disregarded by the world around us. The type of grief I call Invisible Loss is a subtle yet persistent emotion that is not easily defined, especially since we can't explicitly link it to a specific past event. It can surface as a feeling that is commonplace, like anxiety or sadness, angst or restlessness. In essence, it is a form of loss stemming from an encounter that shifts our perception of ourselves. We will be exploring these feelings together: the origin of your Invisible Loss and how you coped along the way. In other words, we will seek to pinpoint the place where you got derailed and ever since, unbeknownst to you, have been living in continuous survival mode. Understanding what, when, and why this Invisible Loss occurred will help you develop self-compassion, which can aid in your healing and comfort you as you recover from this unexpected strain of grief. Once there, you get to find your way to a life of your choosing instead of living a life you must endure.

Our Haven Becomes Our Prison

Before we go any further, it's critically important that you understand that you did what you had to do to get through and survive these veiled hardships of your life. You had no choice but to protect yourself from what we will call a *Moment of Impact* (an emotional punch) that resulted in a world that, at the very least, got confusing and emotionally chaotic. For example, imagine that when you were an early teen, you argued with your mom about her being out of the house all day when all you wanted was to spend that time with her. Or was there ever a time when you felt misunderstood during a meeting at work, and you could not for the life of you explain to your colleagues what you really meant? Maybe you lost sleep over that, replaying how embarrassed and frustrated you felt. As a result, you avoided stepping up again to prevent a subsequent hit. If this wasn't the first time you were misunderstood, perhaps you can't help but feel that this is the "story of your life." We will delve into the feeling of an unending series of these Moments of Impact that will lead us to your Primary Invisible Loss—the loss that created an identity of self that is helpless in the face of that story, and the reason why you have always felt like you needed to guard and protect yourself.

Protecting yourself was necessary, especially when you needed to take a breath after that punch. You took emotional shelter and pulled out of risky choices and life adventures to safeguard your hurt self from additional loss. But what you didn't know then was that this immediate flight to safety wasn't supposed to last as long as it has. The protection you chose for yourself was only meant to help you cope for the first day or two. What nobody explained was that this anxiety you felt in the aftermath of your hurt was the result of actual grief, the kind of grief that had no witness and no label.

This type of sadness comes when we lose faith in ourselves and our abilities. This kind of sorrow can masquerade as your identity, which is perhaps why you don't give it a second thought. An additional characteristic to note is that Invisible Loss is a full-body experience. It can manifest as nausea before a meeting or heart palpitations in the middle of a conversation. These are the symptoms of having survived an invisible moment of loss in the past, but having unconsciously remained in a state of survival beyond it has shifted your thought and emotion regulation from higher-level thinking to a primal response. What isn't clear right away is what this change means for our lives and how it shows up in real, long-lasting ways.

These undeniable changes vary and may be disguised as mundane, everyday dealings. Whether you were trying to express a new idea to your boss or finding the courage to tell your friend that she hurt your feelings, or whether you held back from going after a promotion at work or speaking your mind at home, you blindly stayed in survival mode. But before you knew it, weeks, months, and years went by with you keeping things in, holding yourself back. You made your home there, and you found yourself in a life you did not set out to create—staying in relationships you didn't enjoy. You may have also taken on responsibilities that you never really chose for yourself. This holding-back type of life was only meant to be your chaperone during your guarded moments; you were not meant to live with a warden at the door. But how did it all start? How did your primitive brain begin to take over?

My Discovery

Before I explain how I stumbled on this form of grief and its invisible annihilation of a good life, I should tell you that I was already very familiar with the emotions surrounding "traditional" grief. My own personal life took a very sudden turn in 2003 when my thirty-one-year-old husband was diagnosed with Stage 4 colon cancer. It was almost as if my life before his diagnosis was abruptly halted, with no hope of a restart or a reentry into it. At the time of his terminal diagnosis, our two daughters were nine months and two and a half years old. We had just moved from California to the greater Boston area with no family nearby. After a long and obliterating battle with cancer, we unfortunately lost him, and the girls and I were forced to begin a new life on our own. I spent the first four years after his death just surviving every day the best I could—keeping my head down, doing what had to be done to keep my family afloat.

In 2010, after a period of not only dreading every day but also strongly resenting the aftermath of his loss, I decided to leave my job in the corporate world to write about my personal experience of grief and find a way back to living a good life. I vowed that if I were given another chance at a good life after such a devastating loss, I would find a way to help everyone else who was stuck grieving indefinitely. And so I did. I started bringing together large groups of people. As time went by, I began to notice specific patterns in grieving people across many cultures and all genders and races. I glimpsed the beginnings of what I later called the *Life Reentry Model*®, a method for helping people come back to life after the initial aftermath of a devastating event. I wrote my first book, *Second*

Firsts, in 2013 and introduced my initial Life Reentry methodology to the world. My groups continued to grow, with my mission grounded in helping the bereaved not only find their way back to good lives but also discover who they were without their loved ones.

The initial premise of the method is that, after a tragic loss, the individual is stuck between two worlds, in a psychological, purgatorial space I termed the *Waiting Room.* It is a gap *between* lives: one life has been forced into the past due to a loss, and another has yet to begin. You can think of it as a mindset shift: before an individual can overcome a loss and return to a life of fulfillment, specific changes in mindset must occur. These changes involve allowing suppressed emotions to be shared, processed, and reframed to prepare for Life Reentry and a thriving future. Understandably, overcoming these challenges and rewriting our present and future are easier said than done.

After I'd been teaching the model for a few years, I noticed there was a different kind of past event influencing the recovery from a traditional tragic loss. At first it appeared as a type of "grief trance," where the individual would stare into space while recalling a Moment of Impact from their past but communicate it to the group as if it were still happening. It appeared to be something hidden, untold, veiled from the group participant and from everyone around them. It was a phantom kind of loss—a moment that had impacted the individual but seemed to have remained not only unprocessed but also invalidated and uncategorized. This loss was something our society had never recognized as "real."

The discovery did not feel instant or immediate; rather, it took some time to identify it as an actual loss of self, caused by a painful emotional impact that had happened in the past. At the time, it was misunderstood and perceived as trivial, certainly not considered an actual tragedy. It didn't appear like grief because it had already evolved into what I call a Waiting Room mindset, which was neither defined nor understood as such by our society at large.

This Waiting Room, to which we all eventually find our way, is created early in life, most likely before any tragic loss occurs. It is born with a different form of grief that leaves most of us trapped and continually surviving, *in between* experiences in invisible ways. We may stop fully living much earlier than we think we do; we are trapped for much longer. So when my class participants kept finding themselves in survival mode, back in the Waiting Room without a logical reason, I realized what had really taken place.

To pinpoint the origin of their Survivor mindset, I asked participants to consider what Moments of Impact might have happened *before* the tragedy that took their loved one. Recalling their first foray into the Waiting Room—where they had created this survival mechanism to deal with the possibility of any future loss—was a big challenge at first. But once they tracked down that moment (or moments), they could then start to see a way out. With the tools of the Life Reentry Model, they slowly started to understand what really happened to their emotional well-being and where and when they stopped thriving and, unbeknownst to them, started long-term surviving. This new kind of awareness (the Awareness phase of Life Reentry) allowed them to embark on the path to living a life of choice, not just for brief periods of time but for the long haul. The Life Reentry Model may be the final piece of the puzzle in healing, not only from what is "traditionally" understood as grief (as mentioned, catastrophic events such as the death of a loved one) but also for this more esoteric Invisible Loss of self, which has been chronically misunderstood and may have contributed to many of the mental health issues we grapple with in modern society.

The Reality of Invisible Loss

It is difficult to fathom that suicide is the second biggest cause of mortality among those aged ten to twenty-four. According to the Anxiety and Depression Association of America, "6.8 million American people suffer from generalized anxiety. Women are impacted twice as often as males. Six million U.S. adults suffer from panic disorder. Social anxiety disorder affects 15 million adults and normally begins around age 13, but the majority of sufferers do not seek treatment until much later."[1]

Based on my observations of my class participants over the past decade, it's my firm belief that Invisible Loss is a trigger for anxiety and one of the main sources of depression: society does not validate an Invisible Loss, and consequently, it is dismissed as an unlikely cause of these afflictions.

Looking back, I now see that losing my first husband did not completely obliterate me, as I was afforded some words by our culture to express the bewilderment of tragic grief. At least I was given a basic emotional language to construct a new inner meaning. In time, I distinguished between the bitterness of my fate and the soreness of tragedy. Society partially gave me the permission and space I needed to deal with the surreal aftermath of death. I identified the emotions that arrived, and it meant something to know that my grief was recognized by others: it was certainly not a figment of the imagination of some lost widow.

To be validated, to be told that the depth of my sorrow was worthy of support, saved my life. If only this basic level of validation were offered to Invisible Loss as well. If only this level of regard were present in all our Moments of Impact. If only it were commonplace to process and cleanse our daily sorrows. If only we could be nurtured back to life with proper care. Many lives could have been saved if we had had a simple foundation of validation and acceptance of the different strains of grief.

The acknowledgment of grief is not enough, but it is better than nothing. In my experience, Invisible Loss is silent, unrecognized, and disregarded (not only by society but also by ourselves), as we are unaware of the various emotional states and the range of feelings that it occupies. Depending on when an Invisible Loss takes place, our perception of it and its effect on our behavior will vary. The literal meaning of grief suggests feelings of profound loss and raw emotion—the utter and immediate devastation of the current reality of the mourner. In films, it is always depicted with tremendous emotional outbursts that result in uncontrollable sobbing. This dramatic portrayal of mourning hinders us from recognizing the loss that does not manifest in this way.

In addition, Invisible Loss may be hidden from us and others when it feels more like anxiety than grief. Obviously, it may vary, as each Invisible Loss event depends on the person's circumstances and context. The tricky part is that someone may have the exact same experience as another person, but due to their unique personal circumstances, upbringing, and set of beliefs, it may not qualify as an Invisible Loss for them.

Occasionally, Invisible Loss can be felt in situations when someone is behaving in ways you do not expect. It can also be felt when your version of reality doesn't match up with the version of others. For example, a child may experience Invisible Loss when his mother doesn't act the same way as a friend's mother, causing him to view himself as different. He loses his sense of belonging. This early experience of distinguishing ourselves from what is "normal" produces an inner incongruence. We then adjust our actions and behavior to survive this new experience of conflict by suppressing this feeling without discussing it with anyone.

In other words, Invisible Loss is an acute emotional response to an otherwise normal event. It does not necessarily derive from a traumatic incident or a conventionally labeled instance of mourning. Instead, it's the result of a moment that impacted our sense of self, our understanding of who we are, our self-worth in relation to our immediate surroundings. That altered perception ought to have lasted no more than a few days. Instead, it got buried in the abyss of our inner world, and since it had no permissible outlet for cleansing and processing, the experience that impacted our view of who we are grew more permanent. It was too difficult to revert back to our old perception of ourselves—or the Original Self.

What Is the Original Self?

The Original Self is who we are in the absence of external influence. In other words, it's *you* without the self-correction that occurs when you strive to fit into the mold of your family, community, or social group. It is the self that is most in tune with the experiences that bring you joy. Perhaps the best way to define the Original Self is as the uninhibited version of us, where we are true to our own needs and desires rather than those of others.

This Original Self is not about good self versus bad self or about positive versus negative; rather, it is about making choices based on what is important. If we were to pinpoint the full expression of the Original Self, we would notice an individual form of play, the forging of relationships based on needs (whatever these needs may be), creativity without suppression, and work one loves or chooses to do. When a Moment of Impact takes place—some sort of rejection, either a verbal or nonverbal judgment—that alters our early notion of self, we experience our first Invisible Loss. This Primary Invisible Loss is best described as the loss of who we were prior to that Moment of Impact.

Let's imagine that you experienced a lack of material things early in life, so you could not freely have what others easily afforded for themselves. That could have dictated low self-worth, resulting in a new perception of self that may have changed the way you connected with your friends or formed bonds with others. This perception may have resulted in feeling undeserving of love and forming unhealthy boundaries due to that early loss of value of Original Self.

To survive the aftermath of this loss, you establish a Waiting Room for yourself, as you don't know how to deal with your newly altered self. The longer you stay away from that original version of yourself, the harder it gets to stay true to who you have been. It's like a domino effect. That one early loss of self can be the biggest, most catastrophic event of your life, as everything now is viewed through the optics of surviving that experience and seeing yourself through that lens.

Getting Caught in the Waiting Room

Sometimes there are challenging aspects of our lives that we never question. We simply find a way to endure things without considering the idea that we don't have to work this hard or live this way. Without questioning what is and what has always been, we miss the chance to have an easier life.

Most people think that when something challenging happens to us and we find a way to move on from that experience, we automatically move to a new chapter or a new beginning. We perceive and think of our lives in a linear fashion, as follows:

Old Life → New Life

Hard Moment → Lesson Learned → New Beginning

Since you have not been told that the everyday dread and anxiety you feel may be the result of Invisible Loss, you are also not aware of when or how your survival mechanism was first triggered.

When your survival mechanism was triggered, that old version of you ceased to exist while you were surviving that flash of shame, abandonment, or rejection. As you know by now, we call this a Moment of Impact. Throughout your life, you experience quite a few of these painful invisible setbacks where your Original Self loses faith in its initial self-knowledge. The coping mechanism that your brain devised in reaction to previous Moments of Impact determines how you endure these situations. While that coping mechanism helps you survive, it doesn't lead you to a new beginning; rather, it brings you to a place of safety, a place where you can recover. Therefore, instead of the previously described sequence, the following occurs:

Moment of Impact → Invisible Loss → Survival

You may think you are experiencing a new beginning and you have a second chance at something, but in reality, you are in the space between the old life and the new life, the space between your Original Self prior to a Moment of Impact and your Survivor Self. It's a place of perpetual arrested development, which is what we are now recognizing as the Waiting Room.

The Unexpected Influence of Invisible Loss on Our Lives

Expressing suffering outside of "acceptable" life tragedies (the death of a loved one) and beyond a certain timeline (around six months) is not easily understood by others without some kind of judgment. Additionally, the concept of Invisible Loss has never been expressed with language that can describe it with accuracy; it has been left unsaid and certainly misunderstood, as we usually go where language takes us.

For example, we don't have the language to describe the loss of self-worth that comes from living in a marriage where subtle forms of verbal abuse are embedded in daily conversations. We may not even be aware of the abuse, since that may just be the way we remember our parents talking to one another. Nonetheless, we spend our time holding ourselves responsible for the circumstances in which we find ourselves.

The truth is, it will get worse before it can get better—not only in trying to figure out where your survival of life started but also in how those around you respond to your search. Once others notice you're trying to figure all this out, they'll think you must be having a midlife crisis. How dare you revisit things that are better left unsaid? After all, we are risking the certainty of the familiar understanding of our stories and the comfort we gain from pleasing other people. There will be much more to say about this as we traverse the terrain ahead. You will realize how you created this version of yourself out of necessity and fear of losing love. But now that you're aware of this false self, it's time to say goodbye to it.

And even though we are slowly starting to let go of the way things have been, this is closer to yourself than you have been for a while. Agreeing to the quest for your Original Self may not be simple, but we will gently step inside a brand-new language, one that can define a new future and may even rewrite the past. We will string together words to bring us to new vistas, to dare to ask a different set of questions, pushing out our shame and guilt for the choices we have made thus far. We will come to understand the reasons behind them, which will free us from the chains of regret. Dare I say, by the end of this book, Invisible Loss will not stay invisible. When you create a life that allows for the expression of the unexpressed, ultimately, you will no longer have use for the term *Invisible Loss*. At least, you won't until something else is suppressed; then the term will once again help a new Invisible Loss come into view.

Before we venture much further, I would like to remind you that once we get to a place where you feel free to choose for yourself, you will realize that the journey here was not wasted or lost. As a matter of fact, it will be the reason why you won't quit. It is why you will continue to step forward and keep turning the pages, mindfully working on the suggested homework on your way to a sympathetic view of yourself and others. This next stage of your life will finally be designed by the Original Self, rather than the Survivor Self, which is the voice of fear and speaks the language of the Waiting Room. At last, you will find not only the courage but also the need to reenter a life of your own choosing and experience the joy that comes from the freedom to be oneself. The Life Reentry Model will help you process the Invisible Losses that have accumulated and continue to cause grief. You will create a daily practice for

- Recognizing the voice of fear (Survivor Self)
- Cleansing your Invisible Losses until the mask of the Survivor falls off
- Reframing those fears with wisdom
- Acting with deliberate and planned steps that will strategically place you on the path to saying yes to your own demands versus everyone else's

To sincerely act on one's true wishes is, quite frankly, the only goal worth striving for.

What to Expect
As you move forward, it will be helpful to have an overview of what's to come.

The Life Reentry Phases
In the following chapters, I'll take you through a series of homework exercises that will help you find your way out of the Waiting Room and identify your key Invisible Losses. These exercises are based on the Life Reentry Model, which will lead you toward a new chapter of your life. Here's a basic outline of the journey we will take together:

1. Awareness phase—Origin of the Survivor Self from Invisible Loss. The first two chapters will help you understand how you found yourself in this perpetual survival mode and then walk you to your earliest Waiting Room experience and discover the Invisible Loss that gave birth to it. We will start with the acknowledgment

of the Invisible Loss and its evolution from childhood to adulthood. You will also be introduced to three different personas, or facets of your personality, that exist within you: the Survivor, the Watcher, and the Thriver. Their discovery will make the journey meaningful and easier to complete. It will also change the way you listen to others and understand yourself.

2. Defensiveness phase—Interrupting Survivor thoughts with the Stack. This phase is structured as a Stack of thoughts. It gives you a glimpse of a dialogue that is taking place within. It is a practice that helps you become aware of your Survivor thoughts, which you will gradually reframe toward your original and true sense of self. This phase begins your Daily Stack Practice.

3. Action phase—Exiting the Waiting Room by adding Plug-Ins. Here you'll take small steps out of the Waiting Room beginning with low-risk actions, or "Plug-Ins," that will get you further away from your current automatic fear response.

4. Divergent phase—Shifting through the Watcher Self. As you continue with your Daily Stack practice and your real-life set of newly designed action-plan Plug-Ins, you'll discover the part of yourself that was shadowed. As you start to reveal small portions of your Original Self, you will stumble upon resistance from your Survivor Self and from the people in your life. This phase is all about shifting from Survivor Self to Watcher Self, maintaining the Daily Stack Practice, and being willing to stay out of the Waiting Room for longer intervals with higher-risk Plug-Ins.

5. Integration phase—Recalling the Thriver Self and reclaiming your Original Self. You will start working your way toward the integration of your Thriver and Watcher. Here we will focus on the mindset shifts that are taking place, where you'll get to know your Thriver Self. It is also the time when you will start to believe in this journey and its ultimate destination: your original and true self.

Following the Integration phase, Life Reentry will be complete for the first time. You'll write your life's mission statement, a declaration of this rediscovered, integrated self, where your Survivor, Watcher, and Thriver personas are all working in harmony, making your life fit your newly reactivated Original Self.

There is science behind each step, and I will share a glimpse of it. You don't need to know why something works, but you need to believe that it does so you can commit to the experience of Life Reentry.

The Stories

I am proud of the trailblazers who said yes to the work before it found its way to my first book, *Second Firsts*, and to its clinical trials, way before anyone cared about grief being shared in a virtual setting. Since 2011, it has been my honor to witness thousands of Life Reentries, and I share some of these stories in this book. The names, places, and details are changed to maintain their confidentiality. They have been merged in constructs to safeguard that confidentiality.

I chose stories that stayed with me along the way. The people you will meet have been in my classes. Over the course of a decade, these classes took place first via telephone, then via webinar, then by Zoom, and some in person. Most of the classes had close to a hundred people from all over the world.

Setting Your Pace

All the exercises build on one another. Therefore, the best way to experience this book is to just focus on the page in front of you and the homework in each section (don't skip ahead!). The rule of thumb is just ten to fifteen minutes for each exercise. But it's OK if you choose to read the book in one go and then go back to the exercises after your brain has been prepped for the journey. Or you can go at your own pace and start and stop when you feel it's right for you. The classes took the participants through this process in about nine weeks. You can choose that pace if you wish to and dedicate a week to each phase, or you can take longer to complete the exercises. Consider working through this book with a friend, a family member, or your therapist. Or bring it to your support group. But if these options are not available to you, going through it on your own is perfectly fine and valuable. The book was structured and written specifically for the solo journeyer. The Life Reentry methodology supports you as an individual without the need for a class facilitator, so don't feel the pressure to do this with a partner or a group if you don't want to.

Appendix

The appendix contains both an extensive guide for a support group format and a structured weekly format for the solitary reader.

Working through this book in a support group setting is merely an option and not required; if you find that reading *Invisible Loss* in a support group context is more appealing, please refer to the guide in the appendix.

If you are interested in reading the book in a structured weekly format, the appendix support group guide may be useful to the solo reader as well. The appendix outlines the weekly Life Reentry reading and practice assignments for nine weeks. You may find it much simpler if it has been laid out that way for you. Use the format that allows you to learn best. After all, this book is about the transformation of your life; you ought to make it work for you.

The Life Reentry Glossary

Life Reentry contains its own lexicon, and broader notions will be described in respective chapters and outlines. In addition, to simplify your approach, all the terminology encompassed in Invisible Loss— keywords and concepts—will appear with first capital letters (for example, Invisible Loss or Life Reentry). The glossary of terms provides a list of short and simple definitions.

Coffee Breaks

There is a "Coffee Break" in the middle of each chapter. I wrote these pages as if I were sitting in the chair across from you and we were having a cup of coffee together.

We are, in many ways, outside of time and space, conversing with each other.

I hope these little breaks bring the book to life as you are reading—it is my wish that you feel as if we are in class together. But before we get started, let's end this introduction with your very first homework about yourself and where you are as you begin your Life Reentry journey.

....

Homework: Your Baseline Story of Self

Find a journal, either physical or digital, to use for the assignments that are included in this book. Start your journal with this introductory assignment about how your life story sounds and feels to you in the present. Spend a few minutes writing a couple of paragraphs, or more if you wish, introducing yourself as if you are in class, sharing a little bit about your life with others. This will be our "before" snapshot of the way you perceive yourself and your current and past reality. The language you use to describe your past and who you are can point us toward your Waiting Room and how you have been surviving your everyday life. Your words include hints that can take us to the instances of Invisible Loss that have altered the course of your life.

Start sharing your story from wherever you feel is a natural starting point. It could be about where you were born, who your parents were, or where you went to school. Whatever it is, trust it and write it down.

If you don't know how to begin your introductory story, here are some prompts to help you get going:

- *My story began when . . .*
- *I grew up in . . .*
- *The hardest thing in my life has been . . .*
- *Even though I was raised by great parents . . .*

Once you finish your writing, keep this Baseline Story in a readily available spot, as we will revisit it at the end. This is the beginning of a journey that you will want to chronicle as you progress along the way. Here's to the most unexpected rewrite of your life.

....

Homework: Original Self-Inventory Scale

Before we begin the process of identifying your Invisible Losses, we will take stock of how these Invisible Losses may have affected different aspects of your life. I gathered a series of questions on self-trust, boundaries, and honesty. We will assess your capacity to take risks, whether you have healthy boundaries, and whether you have compassion for yourself and others, among other things. We want to get a feel of where you're starting from. All you have to do is carefully consider the questions below and determine where you have been in the previous year on a scale of 0–3 (not doing well in that area of your life) to 4–7 (doing well) to 8–10 (doing really well). For example, if the issue is self-trust, do you check with others or trust your own judgment regarding the decisions in your life? For this example, let's assume you doubt yourself often but have also trusted yourself once or twice in the last year. Your Self-Trust Scale number is likely to be a 3 or 4: you have concerns about what to do next but exhibit flashes of self-trust. After you write down your number for each question, add up all your numbers and write the total in the blank provided. In order to gain clarity regarding shifts in each category, it is advisable to update the score upon completion of the initial Life Reentry Cycle at the conclusion of the book.

Take a few moments now and ask yourself the following questions to assess your individual scores for each one. In the last year, where do you find yourself from 0 (not doing well in the specific area of your life) to 10 (doing really well)? Please use only one number from 0 to 10.

- Self-Trust: When you had to make a tough decision in the past year, did you feel that you couldn't manage it on your own, or did you find it in yourself to take the step without seeking the perspectives of others? How confident are you in your ability to make decisions regarding the course of your life from 0 (not trusting) to 10 (fully trusting)?

My Self-Trust Number is _____.

- Healthy Boundaries: Do you frequently find yourself in relationships that aren't fulfilling? Can you set limits when people make unfair demands on your time in certain situations? Do you frequently say or do things to satisfy others? How readily do you set limits for yourself at home, at work, and in relationships? What is your current score on a scale of 0 (not easily setting boundaries) to 10 (very easily)?

My Healthy Boundaries Number is _____.

- Self-Acceptance: Is it easy for you to embrace the decisions you've made in the past, or do you find that you are picking yourself apart over decisions you've made that you now regret? What is your current score on a scale from 0 (not accepting) to 10 (extremely accepting)?

My Self-Acceptance Number is _____.

- Radical Self-Honesty: Are you able to be honest with yourself about where you are in life, or do you find that you avoid the truth to self-soothe? How honest with yourself are you? From 0 (not honest) to 10 (very honest), what is your current number?

My Radical Self-Honesty Number is _____.

- The Present Moment: How does the present moment feel for you? If you were to stop and just take a deep breath and feel how it feels to be you in the here and now, how does that feel? Is it easy to be in your life in this moment in time, or is it uncomfortable and hard? From 0 (it feels really hard) to 10 (not hard at all), what is your current number?

My Present Moment Number is _____.

- Giant Leap: In the last year, have you been able to make any giant leaps in your life, like changing jobs or leaving a relationship? These types of changes are the hardest to make, and most of us struggle with them. How easy is it for you to make a big leap toward something you want in your life from 0 (not easy) to 10 (very easy)?

  My Giant Leap Number is ____.

- Compassion Toward Others: Do you feel you have compassion toward others regarding their hardships and misfortunes in life? From 0 (no compassion) to 10 (a lot of compassion), what is your number?

  My Compassion Toward Others Number is ____.

- Compassion Toward Self: Do you blame yourself for any abandonment you may have experienced from others? Can you understand the reasoning behind some of your behaviors that could have hurt others? How forgiving and understanding are you about the perceived mistakes you made or the choices that didn't lead you where you thought they would? What is your score, from 0 (no compassion) to 10 (a lot of compassion)?

  My Compassion Toward Self Number is ____.

Add up all the numbers and write the total score here: *My Original Self-Inventory Score is ____.*

I

Awareness Phase

Origin of the Survivor Self from Invisible Loss

The torture of making a new life may not be as
hard as trying to hold on to the old one.

Awareness Phase
During this phase, you will be looking back at your life story
through the prism of Invisible Loss. You will review your own
Moment of Impact that resulted in your very first Invisible Loss,
ultimately leading to the first experience of the Waiting Room.

Lesson
What is the Origin of the Survivor Self and its
distinct but currently concealed behavior?

Chapter 1

The Waiting Room

We begin our journey in the middle, where we consciously or unconsciously may be stuck between two worlds. This place, as I mentioned earlier, is a psychological space that you entered to protect yourself from an Invisible Loss. It is a gap that can both heal and hinder you, depending on how long you stay when you get there. This holding pattern can feel comfortable, but it inhibits you from living a life of your choosing. Because it feels safe, it can be challenging to find your way out. Most of the time, you don't even know you are an occupant of the Waiting Room. However, as long as you feel threatened by the events of your past, your brain will not be able to devote its attention to future planning. Instead, it will insist on ruminating on what you are weighted down by and what may occur as a result in the future. While in this space, your brain's focus has absolutely nothing to do with what you wish to do or have. In many ways, you are being held captive within it, in a prison that you stepped into voluntarily to survive a Moment of Impact, seemingly unimportant at the time.

What is not rational about this choice up to now is that you didn't think you were surviving anything tragic; you thought this was just another day. These events appeared as run-of-the-mill experiences, but they adjusted your view of self and your perception of how others viewed you. Even though it's hard to imagine, this still put you in a state of survival.

Suppose you discover that your best friend has kept something from you. From then on, whenever you ask her how she is doing, and she appears quiet or tired, you immediately think she is keeping something from you. You don't feel grief; instead, you feel doubt where doubt was not present before. That doubt also creates a loss of certainty about how well you know your friend and leads to a loss of self-trust in your own perception of someone you thought you knew well. Even though you are not directly feeling grief, you are just feeling frustrated about the situation, and you are confused about the kind of relationship you have, this is a loss. Loss is not experienced at the Moment of Impact but rather in its aftermath. And during this longer-term aftermath, you make decisions based on what you believe is happening as opposed to *what really is*. You may leave the friendship thinking that she is not a good friend to you, believing that she abandoned you. You lose that friendship, not because she wasn't a good friend to you but because of your Invisible Loss. I know this partial responsibility for the friendship loss can be hard to accept. Of course, it is not always the case, as many other factors can contribute to the end of a friendship, but when we doubt our relationships, it is important to consider how our Invisible Losses influence our perspective on them.

There is, of course, a neurological explanation for the origin and diligent maintenance of these behaviors. The longer we remain in this safe space, the more we convince ourselves that the comforts of the Waiting Room outweigh any possible benefits we might receive by leaving. We ultimately start to self-identify with this place, incorporating this Waiting Room into our personality and lifestyle, thinking, *This is just life*. But these habits do not reflect your priorities or goals for the future. The Waiting Room is a chronic condition deeply rooted in our brains' evolutionary survival techniques. It can cause long-term cognitive and perceptual changes. It can be challenging to disable, as it is connected to our survival mode. We automatically go inside a safe place while we perceive emotional danger. During COVID-19, for example, as the stress of a pandemic transitioned to a longer-term phase, we grew accustomed to consistently devoting significant mental energy to coping, neglecting important secondary tasks.

To simplify the concept further, let's look briefly at two additional examples of both outward expression and cognitive manifestation of Waiting Rooms.

- Outward Expression of the Waiting Room: Not getting dressed or showered as we used to do every day or ending up with an empty fridge, unpaid bills, unwashed dishes. These new habits start to feel like normal aspects of life. We adapt to not caring for ourselves, not getting adequate nutrition, and it's here that we graduate to the Waiting Room mindset.

- Cognitive Manifestation of the Waiting Room: We start by letting our feelings go unexpressed as we become more focused on maintaining the facade of being "fine" than on addressing our Invisible Loss due to its not being an acceptable loss to grieve. This coping mechanism stems from a prior Moment of Impact and the surviving of its Invisible Loss. Without realizing it, we reintroduce some of our coping habits and self-soothing mechanisms to get us through this period of our life. We then, once again, transition to a longer-term Waiting Room life. A similar aftermath can happen when you stop enjoying a job you once loved. This is the Waiting Room mindset in which you convince yourself that you must stay longer, as you have no other options.

- Outward Expression of the Waiting Room: You start to use food as a self-soothing mechanism. When you get home, you are too exhausted to work out or cook for yourself. You may have stopped going to your book club or calling your best friend on your way home from work. If you are working from home, you barely leave the house, as you use delivery service for groceries and dinner.

- Cognitive Manifestation of the Waiting Room: Your Original Self gets depleted further when you convince yourself to stay at the job because you are really good at it. But you start to drop the ball on certain tasks, and you may begin to experience self-judgment and even hatred. By the time you start to feel that hatred of self, you have already been in the Waiting Room for a while.

Let's now meet Peter and get to know about his discovery of a significant Invisible Loss and how he ended up in the Waiting Room much earlier than he thought he did. As we move forward, we will delve deeper into how the Waiting Room manifests in our lives so that we are better able to recognize it for ourselves.

Peter's Invisible Loss

Peter is a fifty-seven-year-old avid cyclist who rides his bike religiously every Sunday. Seven years ago, he survived cancer, both emotionally and physically, and since then he has been attending a weekly support group. There, he is regarded as someone who defied the odds—as someone whose story of survival inspires. People have come to rely on him as the person who welcomes all the newbies into the group. He is proud to recount the story of his battle with cancer and how he "nearly died on the operating table."

Peter has worked for the same company since 2011, prior to his cancer journey. He lives in a beautiful four-bedroom house that overlooks the lake where, growing up, he spent every summer with his grandfather. After going into remission in 2015, he purchased his home to celebrate the beginning of a new life.

His wife is a high school math teacher who frequently tutors students during after-school hours. Peter volunteers at the local food bank and makes sure he donates to it monthly. He joined my Life Reentry class after a coworker resigned to pursue a career in graphic design full-time.

Peter was curious as to how his colleague had made that decision. After all, his coworker had a family of four to support and had always expressed concern about losing his job. This change was quite surprising to Peter, to say the least.

Call it curiosity, call it destiny. Peter registered for the class. The first class is always on the discovery of our Invisible Losses, as we spend a whole week discussing the nature of what Invisible Losses are and how to track them down. Peter movingly described his experience with cancer and its profound effect on him. How he narrowly escaped death, how he now lives his life with gusto, and how he heard about this class from a dear friend. He thought he would give it a go so that he could recommend it to others.

I asked Peter, "How about you? Is there an Invisible Loss that comes to mind?"

He quickly responded, "No, not really. I am sure others will have plenty to share. You see, going through cancer kind of eradicates all other losses."

"Well, Peter," I responded, "you just take your time with this. When you have a moment to spare, try to recall a time when you were unexpectedly shaken by an event." The class went on, and people shared their uncharted losses. As usual, our online group was filled with hundreds of shares.

Peter stayed quiet. His extroverted support group persona completely vanished. I later received an email stating that he felt that he was not suited for this class and that others needed it more than he did. He thanked me for doing this work and said he would be sure to let others know about it.

I wrote back, sharing with him that the intangible nature of his possible Invisible Loss makes it hard to see at first. I advised him to give it a little more time. If he later decided to move on, I would issue him a refund.

He said he would think about it. Next week arrived, and there he was, his camera off from the Zoom interface but listening to all the other participants sharing their newly discovered losses.

Not a peep from Peter.

Another week went by. Again, he emailed to inform me that his father traveled a lot when he was younger. He never really spent much time with him, but his grandfather was always there to hang out, so he really didn't miss having a father figure in his life. And other people, he added, had it much worse than he did. "Like your kids, their dad passed. At least my father was available on weekends and occasionally during the week. He never beat me. He never yelled at me even. So I am not sure what you are looking for."

I said to him, "I am not looking for anything: you are. And if it's OK, I would like to ask you another question. How did it feel that your dad wasn't around much? For a minute, let's not think about the kids who have no dads and all the unfair things in the world that have happened to other people. I am interested in your experience."

Peter didn't respond to my email for a couple of days. But when he did, he said his dad only paid attention to him when he picked up after himself. He remembered how his dad would always praise him when Peter wiped his mouth and folded the napkin on his lap, or when he cleared the table and loaded the dishwasher. He said it was the only time he felt seen by his dad. He added in the email that, as he was writing this to me, he realized he still did this. Even though his dad was no longer alive, he still did this with his family, especially his wife. He always made sure he did things perfectly when she was around, how she mentioned to Peter that only he knew how to stack their dishwasher. And he always brought her a cup of tea when she needed it, without her even having to tell him. In the email, he expressed his pride in being of service to his wife. He didn't understand why that should be a negative, but in many ways, he did understand how he perceived his worth based on how he served others.

He added that he could also see this same kind of relationship at work with his team and his boss. He was the one cleaning up other people's mistakes, as his boss said that he was the only one he could trust to do it. He always prided himself on that, but he wished he were also being asked to lead a new project rather than clean up an old one.

At the end of the email, he said that he felt he was never valued for anything except for making sure all practical matters were taken care of. That was why being part of the support group had been such a refreshing change for him. People there saw Peter as an inspiration and not as someone who picked up after them.

We went back and forth with a couple more emails, and Peter realized that his Invisible Loss was that he was only seen for his ability to take care of others, not for his ability to inspire. He had lost the sense of self that told him how inspiring he was.

It was the Invisible Loss of an identity of inspiration. He said that he could only see himself as someone of service and nothing else. His Invisible Loss was no longer knowing what else he was good at. His Invisible Loss was not remembering his inspiring (Thriver) part of his Original Self. And that also meant that nobody else knew him, either. In many ways, that self no longer existed. The only part of him that existed was that little boy, picking up after himself, waiting to be rewarded by his father. He said that was his Survivor Self, who made sure he used this part of himself to get ahead in life, as this was the part that was missing from others around him. Nobody was there to clean up, pick up loose ends, and care for others in the way that he did.

Peter came back on camera the next week and shared his revelations with the group. He added that he had suddenly started to see more Invisible Losses. They seemed to have all been hiding under the main one.

His first Plug-In (this is an action that is a small step out of the Waiting Room; I'll elaborate on that in chapter 5) was to not load the dishwasher that evening and to use that time to write his first journal exercise for class, as he had become curious about the guy (Original Self) whom he hadn't been able to visit with for the last fifty or so years of his life.

The life Peter had created was based on what was of value to him as a little boy. It was based on what his father deemed worthy of attention. It was why Peter couldn't see the value in being anyone else or figuring out what else he liked to do or create. It was as if the other parts of him were never born. They were forever lost—never uttered, shared, or shown. They never became real. He remained in a state of potentiality.

Justification of the Life in the Waiting Room

Peter rationalized the means by which he made his living and the manner in which he gave himself value in relationships. Because he had elevated his coping mechanism to a star quality, he didn't realize he was stuck in the Waiting Room. We frequently view our ways of coping as a positive. Certainly not as our demise. There are many lives and many stories that we have not had the chance to live and experience because of many Invisible Losses, especially since new ones are created through Moments of Impact.

Rejection of Life Reentry

Peter tried to deny his need for Life Reentry and at first resisted acknowledging his own hardship. It is difficult to find the words for what was never born or never seen, as there was nothing to mourn or talk about. It doesn't exist in our memory as a grief event. It's not a part of our grief process. It is merely a profound, hidden knowledge waiting to be discovered and given a voice.

I will share more about Peter as we move through this journey together. But this part of his story is a great example of how a seemingly perfect life can shadow the surviving element of your life and hide your lack of thriving. The highest praise from your wife or boss can be your greatest detriment. It appears as a contradiction, as a moment of duality, when we seem to have a good life but what we really have is a shelter protecting us from more pain. That is a central theme of Invisible Loss.

Imagine a life beyond what you have known as "good enough," a life where your Original Self once resided. This is our intended destination, and we are already heading toward it.

How Do We Get Stuck in the Waiting Room?

The majority of people live in a very restricted space, and the best way to illustrate that is with an infinity loop that never ends. Although we are moving, we remain in the same area, almost like being on a treadmill. Survival mode is a loop of thinking that keeps us "busy" but still in one place. In life mode, on the other hand, we change and grow within an expanding spiral.

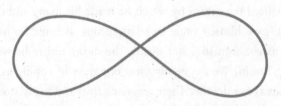

Survival Mode

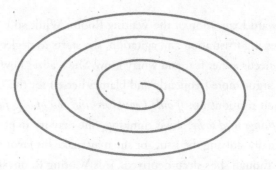

Life Mode

Your survival mode thoughts are created by the way your brain processes certain memories associated with specific events. It can produce responses of fear and joy, as well as influence your future willingness to engage in similar situations. The fight-or-flight response is a well-known behavior. For example, consider someone who appears to have a good marriage, and by outward appearances, she does. But her spouse talks about a specific coworker all the time, while she has been stuck at home with a nine-month-old baby. She tries to shake the thought *My partner is mesmerized with another woman while all I do is take care of our child.* When she tries to talk to her husband about how she feels, he dismisses her feelings and laughs at her for even thinking he's interested in anyone else. This is what that experience might look like through the lens of the Waiting Room:

- Cognitive Manifestation of the Waiting Room: Her Survivor-based narrative loop begins here: *You're overweight. You're unattractive. Your brain no longer functions as it once did. He's going to leave you. You're not worthy of him. Or anyone.* She steps into the Waiting Room in an effort to shield herself from his rejection. She becomes agitated when he asks her a simple question or when he is ten minutes late driving home from work. This agitation does not originate from her Original Self but rather from her Survivor Self, which is trying to shelter her from surviving the effects of seeing her partner's smile while he is speaking about someone else.

- Outward Expression of the Waiting Room: While still expressing frustration and agitation, she starts to neglect her own needs as her fear and worry grow. She realizes now that they argue more frequently and blames herself for this change in their relationship: *If only I could remind you of how fun and easy things used to be,* she is thinking. She may try to please him by totally skirting the issue, or she may make his favorite dinner even though she's sleep-deprived. This Waiting Room she created for herself allows her to deny the truth she is witnessing about her husband's attention to his colleague and to step into the role of caring spouse. She stays there, neglecting her need for connection by denying her intuition for as long as she can, wondering what she's done wrong, and blaming herself for not being interesting enough anymore.

- Cognitive Manifestation of the Waiting Room: Her mind shifts from logical thinking to obsessive worry over abandonment and rejection. While she thinks she's experiencing this for the first time, she is very likely to have had an early experience in her childhood of feeling abandoned.

Reminders of that previous event may activate certain emotions. The brain will try to dumb down the possibility of more loss and ignore the fact that the association between the past and present event is strong. This is how the Waiting Room mindset is created. When an emotion is overwhelming, we tend to justify it or mistake it for a component of our identity. We blame ourselves for the way we feel or fault ourselves for what has taken place in our lives to put us in this situation. We respond to that fear as if it's true.

The Long-Term Lease

The Waiting Room was built with a spectrum of modifications and adjustments in order for you to survive an experience of Invisible Loss. It could be as simple as keeping your hair long to hide your face because you grew up believing you didn't look good since you had acne as a teenager.

Or, on the other end of the spectrum, it could be the feeling of rejection when, as a kid at school, you didn't have any friends to sit with during lunch. As an adult, you doubt yourself when you don't get invited to meetings. Your job pays well and it provides for your family, but it puts you in survival mode, trying to cope with that same Invisible Loss. The loss of not being wanted. Not being seen. Not chosen. You blame yourself for the decisions made by your boss not to give you that raise. So you stay at that job since the Survivor narrative has you believing that nobody else would hire you. *You are lucky they hired you in the first place. After all, many would do anything to have this kind of job.* You continue to work at a job that doesn't value you. You self-soothe with an extra drink before bed. The secret binge-eating. The Netflix weekend binge.

The Waiting Room life makes it feel safer to live in this unviewed cycle of inner life than to even consider disclosing it to yourself. When everything looks the same to anyone on the outside, yet everything has changed on the inside, we go into the Waiting Room to live our lives. We feel broken, and we remain in this feeling of brokenness. Just because this is not considered a big tragedy or a tough divorce doesn't mean we are not grieving the life we could have had. Grief from tragic loss feels raw and relentless. Grief from Invisible Loss at first may feel like anxiety, shame, or embarrassment. It feels more like grief in the latter part of the journey once we become aware of the Invisible Loss.

These losses, sure, don't look like what you'd expect. But they add up. They combine. They conglomerate and congeal. They become the Waiting Room, which hides on the edge of your peripheral vision. These Waiting Rooms make their homes inside hiding places that are often found in unhealthy relationships, in the choices you make with food, in daily alcohol consumption, in procrastination, in lack of self-care. But they also appear in beautiful gardens, in pristine homes, in blessed motherhood, in wealth, in middle class, in big families, in so many ways you can't possibly imagine. The list is long. But as we move forward, you will start to understand how, for example, wealth, pristine homes, and gardens can have a Waiting Room in hiding.

Origin of the Waiting Room and Birth of the Survivor Self

How did the Waiting Room first get created? How did you consciously choose to survive versus thrive? How did your Original Self get rejected? Let's go back in time and piece together all the information we have gathered to see how this may have played out in your life.

Let's say your Original Self had fun playing in the yard, losing itself while processing something challenging. As a kid, you acted out the pain you felt, and nobody seemed to notice or say anything about it. So you advised your toy soldiers to keep going strong while in the battlefield. Or while having tea with your dolls, you revealed what was really troubling you through the doll's voice. You incorporated it into the play's narrative.

You then added all the other confusing emotions you were feeling (more early Moments of Impact) as they were coming in. But there came a time when playing your way through these moments was not enough to get you through. You were no longer a young child allowed to play for hours, processing these invisible, hard experiences. You created this part of you (the Survivor Self) to protect yourself in the combat zone, to sing you a lullaby when you cried yourself to sleep. This Survivor Self was born to surround you with experiences that didn't frighten you. It made a home for you, a safe haven while you were sad, so you could wait out the storm. And that is when the Survivor Self built your first version of the Waiting Room. Think of it as a play tent where you went and hid from the monsters. Inside that Waiting Room, the Survivor Self made sure you were being held and supported during those tough times. After a while, you grew up, had your first relationships, and had to leave that Waiting Room to go out into the world for a bit so you could experience something new.

The Survivor Self came along, granting you full access to your coping mechanisms. When your new high school crush was breaking your heart by flirting with your best friend, your Survivor Self would whisper in your ear that you didn't need this relationship after all, and you would self-sabotage. Sometimes you would come across as an arrogant, spoiled brat as the Survivor found its voice and spoke out of your mouth. But just like you grew, it grew too. As life became riskier, the voice of fear beckoned you back, reeling you into the Waiting Room. There are a few different paths that the Survivor Self might take you down to get you to the Waiting Room. And some of these methods will keep you confused for longer than others. The following are some examples of what some of these may look like:

- The What-Ifs: More and more Moments of Impact came, and as you were able to make your way back to that Waiting Room with greater and greater ease, the Survivor Self voice started to resonate as it echoed within you, and so you made it your own. Pain and loss of any kind, big or small, prompted the Survivor to wrap its arms around you and tell you to be afraid of the storm that *could* come. The people who *could* hurt you. The love that *could* break you. The job that you *needed* to keep. The relationship you needed to stay in because it was safe. The responsibilities. The burden you had to keep carrying.

- The People-Pleasing: Perhaps you felt a sense of obligation to adopt a subservient role, such as becoming the person who always tried to keep everyone happy, ignoring your personal needs and wants so you could be a part of a group, a community, an accepted family member, and so on. Fitting in felt like imprisonment, but you felt as if you had no choice but to alter yourself. The Survivor Self convinced you that this was the only option if you wanted to belong.

- Life's Tragedy: When something crushing hit you, like the death of someone you loved, or the divorce from the love you thought you had, or the layoff from that job that kept you paying the rent—well, when that happened, you were pushed so far inside that Waiting Room (with the Survivor Self yelling at you, *Run fast, come here*) that true healing became almost impossible.

- The Takeover: You continue to go inside the Waiting Room to put yourself back together just as you always did, but when you endure a more severe blow, you stay longer and longer.

Eventually, the Survivor Self takes over every part of your day: how you do your morning and night routine, how you show up in your day with the people in your life. Everything now is done with the Survivor Self whispering in your ear, coaxing you to languish inside the comfort of the Waiting Room.

To further simplify the concept of the Waiting Room, so that you can distinguish between the Survivor Self and the Waiting Room, think of the former as fear-based thoughts and the latter as the behavior (resulting from mindset) and action (outward expression of manifestations of being stuck in the Waiting Room) stemming from those Survivor-based thoughts. The longer we spend surviving an Invisible Loss, the bigger the Waiting Room gets, and the further away from our Original Self we go. After a while, you forget where you are. You forget that this is not your life, that it is just a comfort space, and you stay there for days, for months, for years, for decades, until the last day. And we don't want to get to that last day and realize where we really have been all along. This is why we are choosing to give ourselves the chance of looking for the Moments of Impact, finding them, and seeing them without the Survivor's eyes.

In order to do that, let's now identify what the components of the Survivor Self are, the language it employs, and the script that is mostly thrown at you. Believe it or not, I have discovered over the years that our Survivor Selves are similar across cultures, nations, and age groups. The general language, the messaging of the Survivor brain, is more or less the same for all of us regardless of our origin story, but it is indeed possible for us to overcome that messaging and rewrite it all together.

Language of the Survivor Self

The Survivor Self has a particular language and vocabulary in which it responds to external stimuli. It filters the incoming information from others by looking out for threats and dangers.

- Establishing Threat: The Survivor Self often worries about making decisions in everyday situations where there is no external conflict or a high-level threat (for example, *If I tell them what I really think, they won't like me*).

- Internal Playacting: The Survivor voice is constantly drowning out your logic and your playfulness. It acts out the worst-case scenario, convincing you that the action you are considering is not going to end well: *Don't even try to say anything; you know better than that.*

- Self-Soothing: When we are anxious about a possible future event, we frequently self-soothe by consuming rather than creating—for example, by binge-eating or watching excessive amounts of television. We also choose to self-soothe as opposed to experiencing something new outside of our familiar daily routine. Let's remind ourselves that for the Survivor, comfort is always the top priority.

- Looping: Survivor-based thoughts are on an infinite loop—no matter what takes place externally, it never changes. It delivers the same response to a question no matter what the question is. It often sounds like *I am not ready to do this. This is too hard for me. I don't know. I'm not ready. I don't care anymore. I don't know what I want. I'm always tired. No one understands. I'm afraid to. I can't cope. I'm overwhelmed. I've tried. What's the point? It's not going to work.*

- Misreporting: You may feel unseen and not understood even when others may not necessarily show behavior of judging or ignoring you. The Survivor Self will search for evidence to prove that this judgment from others toward you is accurate.

Rest assured that you will get a chance to look for these behaviors in your own life a little later in this chapter. For now, let's take a quick coffee break for a breather and to feel our feelings.

Coffee Break

It is a tough competition between having a self-soothing evening after work and being here with me, working through an inner war between your past and current selves. The good news is that you are not the only one here. There are others reading this very page, wondering the same things.

So look around you in this virtual room. There are other chairs next to yours. Folks just like you are finding their own place in the room we are in for the long journey into a new chapter. Some are much older than we are, and others much younger. They come from all races and places around the globe. They have strangely different yet comparable stories.

As you've learned by now, there are some key components to the makeup of an Invisible Loss that need to be spelled out and used as a new template, as a new container for the questions and the quest for the best life you can possibly live. Imagine that we are looking at a puzzle. Every piece we put in place brings us closer to the whole. If we don't find all the pieces, we can certainly see the whole picture, but it would be more satisfying to have most of them.

However, we will take whatever we can get.

At first, it will feel as if you can't see anything, just like it feels when you go from light to dark; your eyes must get used to the darkness before you can see. This is the same thing: You are walking in with a perceived sense of self that has been with you for many years. You will witness the Survivor Self hanging on in a stubborn way. Sometimes it will feel impossible to discard it. But it *is* possible, as long as you believe that there is another truth to be revealed by your Original Self. As long as you know you are asleep, then you can find your way to waking up.

Now let's go back to getting to know where you've been so you can design where you can go. Let's see how you introduce yourself at the beginning of this journey. Imagine that we are in class together and you share with the group a few things about yourself. What would you share? Write a few words in your journal about why you are here and what needs to be expressed before you start tracing your Invisible Losses.

Homework: Trace the Invisible Loss in Adulthood

Now that you have spent a little time writing about your life, let's step in a little closer and look at it from the vantage point of impact starting from the present moment going back a couple of years. In this exercise, there is no need to go too far back, as we will look at your Invisible Loss timeline beginning from your early childhood in the next chapter. Think of it as two different starting points that will merge into one timeline where you get to follow the footprints from the present to the past and vice versa.

In this exercise, you will spend a few minutes tracing the evolution of the Primary Invisible Loss and how that has shown up in your adult life. For example, you will be looking for how you are routinely living your everyday life and what you notice about your behavior patterns. The Moments of Impact that put you in grief have created a cluster of behaviors that are interlinked. They stem from a Primary Invisible Loss, which has generated a Survivor-based behavior.

Tracking a Recent Moment of Impact

We will use the following five Survivor-language indicators to spot the behavior and emotional response in order to track the most recent Moment of Impact that is connected to an experience of Invisible Loss.

1. Establishing Threat: Where in your everyday life do you pull back from sharing your thoughts with others? Look at your ordinary routine-based behavior toward family dinners, social gatherings, or when you spend one-on-one time with your partner. The Survivor Self hides in the mundane and everyday details. Write down all the places in your life you would rather not participate in because you (Survivor) have established that it would be emotionally draining, hurtful, or triggering. Start with looking at your close relationships, and then go to professional, community-based, or even social media connections. Open your journal and jot down what comes to mind. It could be as simple as *I feel anxious when I am at dinner with my dad every Sunday.*

2. Internal Playacting: Now that you have jotted down what feels like a trigger or a subtle threat, write down what Survivor thoughts take place during the dinner with your dad. It could be something like *He is going to want to tell me about his new girlfriend and how great she is again, and I have to look as if I am not bothered.*

3. Self-Soothing: Notice how you spent your time (outward expression of the Waiting Room) prior to the event. How did you try to alleviate the anxiety or subtle discomfort you were feeling? You may have snacked on the cookies in the pantry or chosen not to get work done as you had planned. Procrastination is a form of self-soothing. What else did you postpone that the Survivor Self decided was not that important to attend to before your dinner?

4. Looping: Now listen in and spot the Survivor thought that keeps repeating. Write it down even if you feel unsure that it's correct.

5. Misreporting: What is the overall message of the looped Survivor thought? What is it trying to tell you? How is it trying to protect you from the upcoming threat? Is it saying that you will not enjoy your visit with your dad? Is it trying to convince you to cancel?

Identifying the Moment of Impact Event

Now that you have found the behavior of the Waiting Room, can you remember if there was a Moment of Impact event that triggered your entry into the Waiting Room? For example, was there an argument with your dad in the last couple of years where you were hurt or rejected by him? Jot down a short summary of that main Moment of Impact. This is a Moment of Impact that is connected to an earlier Invisible Loss as well as your current Invisible Loss of feeling that you don't have a good relationship with your dad anymore. In addition to writing down that Moment of Impact memory, record your Invisible Loss, Invisible Loss of Self, and Waiting Room behavior. Here is an example:

MOMENT OF IMPACT: A few years ago, my dad and I had a bad argument about how he was treating my mom. Before that argument took place, even though my relationship with him was not great, I used to really enjoy my time with him.

INVISIBLE LOSS: When I don't cancel and still visit with him, our conversation is either about his new girlfriend or the news on TV. It makes me sad as I feel rejected by him. I miss our old conversations.

INVISIBLE LOSS OF SELF (POSSIBLE EARLY INVISIBLE LOSS): I miss being his little girl. I no longer feel special.

WAITING ROOM BEHAVIOR: I now never share my feelings with him; I certainly don't tell him I miss him.

Spotting Behavior Patterns

Now that we've discovered a recent Invisible Loss and how it feels and behaves in your life, can you spot that same behavior in another relationship (for example, with a friend, your boss, or your partner)? Do you also not share your thoughts with them because you try to avoid hurt or rejection, even an argument, without a shred of proof as to a real threat? Write down anything that comes to mind. Please use the template from *Identifying the Moment of Impact Event* segment each time you are trying to spot these behavior patterns.

Chapter 2

The Fragmented Self

Survivor, Watcher, Thriver

In the 2010 movie *Inception*, Leonardo DiCaprio's character enters people's subconscious minds, finding his way inside the dream within the dream, implanting an idea. When he tries to access his wife's mind, you hear him say, "She had locked something away, something deep inside. A truth that she had once known but chose to forget. And she couldn't break free. So I decided to search for it. I went deep into the recess of her mind and found that secret place. And I broke in."[1]

We will break in together, looking for that secret place where your truth lives. This chapter is about getting to know the parts of you that have been hidden and separated from you, resulting in the loss of the Original Self. Not only do we have to find these missing parts, but we also need to figure out the cause of the initial fragmentation. Once that is done, you can then put the newly discovered parts to work and draw upon the wisdom you've gathered over your lifetime while at the same time bringing back that inner kid you left behind all those years ago. By now, you have shared a little bit about your story in chapter 1, and you have a basic description of what an Invisible Loss is and how the Survivor Self plays an important role in its inception. You know the Waiting Room is created by that Survivor Self to protect you from further hurt. In this chapter, you'll be introduced to the other parts of yourself, the Watcher and Thriver, and learn how they can ultimately be your guides out of the Waiting Room as you start to witness the past from a different perspective.

Origin Story and Invisible Loss

Even if you are not religious, our society is largely founded on Judeo-Christian traditions, and the story of Genesis pervades our collective psyche. Shame was born inside the Garden of Eden, where the good world created by God was lost due to human sins. The text points the finger at a pair of original people, Adam and Eve, who had it all and lost it all.

Whether or not you believe the story, that perception endures, the sense that we are living in a shadow world, at a distance from paradise, from wholeness. And we blame ourselves (Survivor narrative) for this alienation. Because even though we were born in a perfect world, we sin and can't help ourselves. We end up spoiling God's good creation. Some Invisible Loss comes from the shame of our own choices in life or from our guilt for the mistakes we made, knowing they cannot be unmade. The harshest Invisible Loss comes from things we have done that have taken us out of our own Garden of Eden.

Disobedience—as a child, as a teen, as an adult in the world of work and home—is an act that creates invisible suffering. We learn to survive that repeated pattern of being commanded by our elders to be "good." In order to be good and obey, we may create a life closer to that command but further away from our Original Self. We may work hard trying to be good, trying to please and fit into the mold created for us, but that only helps to build our Waiting Room life.

But time in the Waiting Room doesn't need to last forever. And you don't have to die inside it. There are parts within you that can bring forth a life worthy of your human existence. Places within yourself that have no shame.

They are intact but silenced. They are strong but have been weakened. They are memorable but have been forgotten so you could survive the aftermath of your hardships. True resurrection of self will destroy you before it can bring you back to life.

Over the years, while working with people on confusing and uncharted loss, I have witnessed the struggle people undertake to be still long enough to start the walk into the mind's battlefield.

The Waiting Room's familiar anchor pulls at them. It becomes clear that it was tolerated, that the Waiting Room was considered better than having to come face-to-face with liberating thoughts and our Original Selves. In the pages ahead, there will be some turbulence because your brain is going to dread the fight among the three selves that is necessary for Life Reentry.

To reestablish the free will of the Original Self and be given the chance at a life of your true liking, your attachment to the artificial peace that your Waiting Room offers will have to end. You will have to make hard decisions. I am not asking for heroics, but it will entail sacrifice. For example, you may struggle with being singled out by your friends or family members when you start to course-correct. Your choices may not be favorable to others, and you may lose that sense of belonging that the Waiting Room life has accomplished for you. It can feel chaotic at first, and you will miss the comfort of your old Waiting Room life. Metaphorically speaking, you will feel homeless, and the Original Self at first will come across as foreign and unfamiliar.

Asking you to sit in your suffering may seem like asking you to jump in the fire and expecting you to not get burned. Slowing down the pace of surviving is necessary. Most Waiting Rooms have us burned out with the wrong actions, the wrong turns and twists. Taming the Survivor can happen only with contemplation. Invisible Loss can't be deleted or obliterated, but it can be guided to a peaceful state of existence by anchoring it there while you sit with it, paying attention to what is true and what is a lie. A lie that was told to you for your own survival, which led to the fragmentation of the self. Without that lie, that fragmentation would never have happened. But let's take another breather and process what we just talked about.

Coffee Break

Are you wondering how you believed the lies, how you listened to the thoughts that convinced you to not try out for that race in high school? You assumed *you wouldn't stand a chance.* You denied yourself asking for help when you needed it most because you *didn't want anyone to think you were not strong enough.*

The Survivor voice mimics your own. You believe it's your thoughts, your free will. The disguise is so successful that it fools not only everyone who sees and hears it, but it also fools you, which is heartbreaking.

All that you thought you knew, but didn't, makes your heart heavy. It is as if you are carrying a whole *arena.* One that no one can see.

There is no witness to it. We all suffer the unvalidated hurts quietly unless—well, unless someone can sit with us. And as we sit together, the *arena* of hurt transitions from the unseen to the seen. I am sitting with you so that you can find the words to share all the moments you thought were not worth sharing.

Especially those.

This is why a good friendship can save your life. A kind stranger can free you. To be seen from the inside is the most healing experience we can ever have. When I write to you about your hidden arena, I am also revealing mine. You see, we save each other this way.

Even just the act of sitting next to each other is deeply felt. It is an act that can lift the pain from your heart once and for all. But there is a very old friend within you who is waiting to be remembered and to find their way back to sit next to you. The timing is right, since you have now learned about the reasons why the Survivor's Waiting Room is created, how that Waiting Room shows up in your everyday life, and the narrative that supports its existence and longevity. Next let's find the part of you that can help you shift out of that Waiting Room. Let me introduce you to the Watcher Self, the good old friend.

The wisest part of you.

The Birth of the Watcher Self

When you were born, you arrived with a witness behind your eyes, an unwavering presence watching everything you do and everything that happens to you. It collected all the memories in a scrapbook, like a parent would. It watched your very first step; it heard you say your first words. It cried when you did and knew why you were so very sad. It witnessed all the events that were both hard and easy but that you were too young to remember.

It was the witness and memory-keeper of every second of your life. It took your memories and made them into inner knowing. It took the aftermaths of hard moments and gave them insight. It then put it all in a safe place inside you for when you would need it in the future. It knows your thoughts, and it can recall all the events that brought you to them. It loves you unconditionally because it understands you better than anyone else. It goes with you wherever you go.

Because of its long history with you, it has all the answers. Every single one of them. The Watcher smiles and remains patient and unwavering in its belief that you will soon look for the answers within. It never stops believing that you will remember your knowing, as it stands next to all of your truths. It has even given all your truths names and ages, as some of them have been there nearly as long as the Watcher.

Let's go back in time a little to look at when you experienced your first Invisible Loss and your sense of Original Self hid from you; you had no idea what it tried to tell you because the whisper of its voice did not have enough volume to make it through the chaos the Invisible Loss brought into your day. The Watcher has always witnessed you feeling the cold, the tsunami, the thunderstorms, and all that the sky brings down on you. It has seen you walking on life's road regardless.

Even though you have forgotten some of the highlights of your life, even though you have been told that these parts of you are no longer there, the Watcher is here to give you the proof that they are. It holds all the fun memories, the photographs that span each second of your existence, and of course all the narrative you expressed originally, without the Survivor's influence.

The Survivor often takes over, but the more we learn to recognize the signs of the Survivor Self, the more we will be able to interrupt its loop of thought. The more we can remember our own wisdom, the sooner we can rewrite that inner conversation in a process called *reframing*.

The Watcher Self has been waiting for you so it can tell you more about the part of yourself that it occupies. Religiously. Spiritually. Metaphorically. Lovingly.

Unconditionally.

But most of all, timelessly.

You are now starting to become better at understanding the narrators of your life, thanks in part to the losses you have experienced. You will start to see how your identity was reconstructed, rooted in the avoidance of pain, and invisibly bound in survival territory that spins itself as a safe place.

But you and that Watcher behind your eyes can shake the foundation of survivorship so hard that the Waiting Room walls will start to crack, and you won't forget where you truly are. The Watcher can make the Survivor sweat buckets, and that is why the Survivor will do everything it can to sabotage the Watcher's reentry. It is important to start connecting with your Watcher early in this process, which is the reason this next visualization exercise is placed right here: to allow you to remember what it felt like to know yourself, to trust your own wisdom, and to believe that you can make the right choices. This exercise will take just three minutes or so, and all you need is a comfortable chair where you can close your eyes and relax your body. First, read the instructions carefully so you can guide yourself through it. You will be asked to connect with the memory of someone who has always trusted your advice and wisdom. This could be a person who is still living or not. It is more about how they made you feel about yourself, mostly about that Original Self that is currently shadowed. The purpose of this visualization is to find the Watcher voice from an external source so it can help trigger and activate the internal Watcher voice. If this doesn't happen the first go-around, make sure you find time for another try.

Have a notepad close by for when you are done with the exercise. You will jot down what you experienced and what you remembered about yourself that you had forgotten. So go get that notepad and come back to your chair so we can begin.

Homework: The Watcher Visualization

First, sit comfortably and calmly while taking deliberate, deep breaths—as many as necessary for your body to release all Survivor-related anxieties. Unwind your body from head to toe. Relax your head, your arms, and your legs. Your body is sensing that you are letting go. *You are safe.*

Allow yourself to recall an image and the energy of a person you love and care for and who really cares for you. This person could be anyone with whom you feel safe.

This person should be someone who always made you feel good. It could be your partner, your child, your teacher, or your mentor. In your mind's eye, start going for a walk together. Somewhere you always liked going in the early years of your life. Take in the surroundings as you are walking together. Notice how it feels to be in that old space that you used to love with the person you have missed. Now notice the loving gaze this person gives you. They are as eager to reconnect with you as you are with them. They bring with them a sense of peace and timelessness.

Now imagine this caring person reminding you of a time in your life when you swiftly made choices for the betterment of all involved. How you had certainty every step of the way, even when it was not clear what needed to take place next. You knew. And you did. Whether you decided on what to do next or whether you needed to stop doing something that no longer served you. This caring friend is reminding you of a moment in time when you simply showed up in your truth.

And it is exactly what you need to hear.

For example, you may need to hear that you are capable and strong or that you're beautiful inside and out. This individual knows the truth of your character and your abilities and wholeheartedly believes in you. When you imagine this person saying the words to you that you have asked to hear as a reminder of who you are, you feel nurtured. Allow yourself to feel love being given to you deeply in your soul. If this person could describe your most important truth and how you need to use it every day, what would they tell you? Imagine yourself being instructed by this loving companion. Listen to what they are saying.

Soak it in and savor it. This message is your truth. Before you end the visualization, it's important to take a moment to feel grateful for the companion who knows you and guides you so well. Feel the kindness that your caring friend holds for you. Express your appreciation.

Then, claim yourself and the gifts you carry within. See yourself doing all that you have been afraid to do, and feel the emotion of this amazing new experience you're having. Take a deep breath in and out, open your eyes, and come back to the present moment. If you begin crying when you do this kind of visualization, that's OK. These tears come from the fountain of your soul, from a place within that remembers who you are and wants to bring you forward into the life you deserve. Such tears are here to awaken the part of you that has the strength to ignite the fire of life that is dormant within you.

Sit back up and savor the moment. When you are ready, write down the truth of yourself that you were reminded of and how it made you feel.

Journal entry prompts:

- *I was reminded of . . .*

- *I found myself remembering how confident I used to be when . . .*

- *I was surprised to be greeted by my old schoolteacher . . .*

- *I felt as if I knew what needed to be done about . . .*

Often during the Life Reentry process, we wonder if the thoughts we are starting to have are really based on our wise old Watcher or on the sneaky Survivor. This questioning is coming from (you are guessing correctly) the Survivor trying to keep you away from change. You may need to write down a reminder in your journal: "Trust the new thoughts that are here more than the ones you are used to." The longer you trust the Watcher thoughts, the easier this part will become and the less you will question them. It's important to write down the truth you are discovering through this process and certainly through the Watcher visualization exercise. Below is a list of some of the distinct ways in which the Watcher could be revealing itself to you in the days following the visualization.

....

Ways the Watcher Makes Itself Known

What you need to remember is that the Watcher never makes a big entrance; the voice is very quiet at first, like the faintest whisper. It is likely that you have not heard your voice of reason for quite some time, and you may not recognize it. It could look like one of the following:

- Increased self-care: All of a sudden, you find yourself simply wanting to make your bed in the morning. You may be thinking, how does that translate as a wise old voice? It is about wanting to occupy a good and nurturing space. Or you may find yourself taking time for a short walk to sort through your thoughts instead of what you normally experience, which is a hurried pace while running errands in between work projects and picking up your kids from day care. These are signs that your Watcher is giving you advice and helping you be more mindful.

- Increased willingness to venture out of your daily routine: You may find yourself doing something unexpected on a Tuesday afternoon. Something like picking out a plant at the grocery store. Simple. Seemingly insignificant. But deeply relevant to you listening to a voice that directs your attention to something beautiful in the midst of the mundane and anxious moments of your life.

- Increased feeling of self-worth: Suddenly you may notice that you say no to something you would normally just do because you could. Maybe your sister asks you to pick up milk on your way to her house. You decide to not go out of your way, even if it would have taken you merely an extra two minutes to get that milk for your sister. It is not that you can't or that you shouldn't; it is that you also don't have enough milk in your own fridge, so you realize that making time to get this for her and not making time to do this for yourself is not logical anymore. So you put your own milk on your list for tomorrow's run at the market. And you leave your house not a minute too early for that visit to your sister's. With no milk. And that feels just fine for the first time.

- Increased self-love talk: You realize out of the blue that you deserve to have a say in conversations with your siblings in regard to what to do with your father's house after his passing, or in what you want for dinner on a Friday night after a long week at work instead of just eating whatever your kids want to have. You have never liked spaghetti and meatballs, and all you crave on a Friday night is that specialty pizza from the brick-oven restaurant down the street. Your Survivor Self will call you selfish, but you will remind yourself of that conversation with that old friend who told you how selfless you really are.

- Mention of new dreams or old dreams: You may find that you drop an old hobby into a conversation with your colleague at work, surprising yourself. Take note. This is no accident; it is not meaningless. It is your old Watcher voice waking up.

Caria's Story

Let me introduce you to Caria.

She decided to register for the Life Reentry class on a whim. In her introductory post, she shared that she was ten years old when she moved to the United States from Turkey. She spoke very little English at that age. She experienced daily bullying but was told at home that it was something she should stop complaining about.

She was often told not to be ungrateful for all the sacrifices her family had made for her. Her mother would bring up examples of family friends who did not have the "opportunities" that she did. How she was one of the lucky ones to be there, in Chicago.

Caria learned very quickly that silence was the desired response at home. She started hiding her day-to-day school life from her parents. Survivor told her it's best not to complain, and she would be rewarded for toughness. Meanwhile, at school, Caria spent lunchtime alone in the cafeteria. She made no friends throughout her middle and high school years. But in college, she got a science scholarship. By age thirty-five, she had received her PhD and gotten a job as a college professor. She was admired and loved by her students.

But Caria was a loner. She spent every night in her small apartment, keeping herself busy with student homework, working all hours.

She proudly shared that she was the first person in her family to go to college. Her mom had passed, but her dad was still there, cheering her on and always describing her as a tough girl who did extraordinary things for her family.

Caria was also her dad's caregiver and supported him financially. She visited him at their family condo, the same one they had moved into twenty years prior. She cooked for him for the week and made sure his laundry was done.

One of her Invisible Losses, she said, was that nobody really knew her. One evening in our group session, she commented that she had considered taking her life at one point. She added that it was just a short moment; it came and went. Almost as if it didn't happen.

Once we shifted gears toward the cleansing exercise (upcoming in chapter 4), looking for the voice of the Survivor Self, she immediately stopped sharing. She disappeared from the public forum of the class.

This was not the first time I had seen this sudden change. In every class, a handful of participants out of a hundred stop sharing once they pass the second week, as it is harder to step into the more action-oriented part of the Life Reentry process. This part requires the unsettling of the old, the questioning of what we think we know, and the last thing we expect when we try to change our lives is to go against the parts of our lives that kept us sane.

Caria wrote to me privately to tell me that she wished she had known about my work in her late teens and early twenties, when she was without any friends at school, struggling to find her identity, but now, even though she felt some loneliness and misidentification from others, she was happy with her life. She loved her apartment and her students. She was grateful that she was financially stable and supporting her dad. She could not imagine a better life for herself. Romance was not something she was interested in, even though her dad wanted grandkids. She didn't believe this was for her, but she could see how important the class was for others who had suffered "real loss."

I decided to give her additional permission to write from the Survivor Self: "Write out what your day was like yesterday and try to 'complain' a little. I want to read your 'complaints.' All of them. As many as possible, Caria, share with me what stands out the most."

I could tell she didn't want to do it. She didn't get back to me for a few days.

I thought I'd lost her. It was clear that her Survivor Self had managed to disguise itself as Caria, and the Watcher Self had become dormant under the Survivor's illusion of safety and familiarity.

But she did respond. At first, she just shared how she was very grateful for the opportunities offered in her life after her parents were brave enough to move to the US. How could she ever complain after their sacrifices? How ungrateful would that make her?

Then she proceeded with this:

"But . . . this morning I didn't want to get up and go in to work. My colleague was having an engagement party at the restaurant across the street after work, and I just didn't feel like going. I got her a gift card the other day, but she insisted I be there tonight. I hate these kinds of gatherings; everyone seems so fake anyways. What is the point? I am not really close with her, and she won't miss me if I am not there. I hate being pressured to show up when I would rather just go home and watch Netflix after being on my feet all day, teaching these kids things they don't want to learn."

She went on and on about how tired she felt in the morning, how she dreaded the whole day. It wasn't just the engagement dinner for her colleague.

I asked her to see what was being revealed through her Cleanse (a written transcription of unfiltered thoughts). Was anything surprising?

I also told her to look for the part of the Cleanse that kept her protecting herself from hurt. We are never looking for our own (Original) voice in the Cleanse, only the Survivor one. Separating ourselves from the nagging, anxious, and repetitive fearful and "complaining" voice is key to recognizing it and bringing it forth.

It is not us (Original Self) that we seek to reprimand or tell off for the complaining or the extreme nature of safety-seeking. It is that inner caregiver and protector (Survivor) that we look to unveil so we can find our way to recognizing the part of ourselves that comes from fearing more pain and more risk.

Caria said that her Cleanse showed she was not enjoying her work as much as she thought she did, but that couldn't be true. Because she did enjoy it. She indicated that her Cleanse was a lie, as she had spent the last ten years of her life loving being a professor and all the accolades she had received. She was shocked that she was not really that eager to go to work and said that I should not take this Cleanse seriously. She was just having a bad day, and that was all there was to it.

I asked her to try to do one of these Cleanses every day that week to see if it was just one bad day at work or more than one.

By the end of that week, she discovered for the first time that her job was not as dreamy as her Survivor Self had told her it was. She started to figure out that her career was mostly based on rewarding her parents and not herself. She had buried herself under the identity of her parents' sacrifice.

Her Survivor almost sounded like her father, who always told her how pleased he was with her life choices and how she had made her grandparents proud, as well as all her aunts and uncles. Every time she went back to visit Turkey, she was celebrated. This identity was a big deal for her family. But deep down, it was not what she needed for herself or who she was.

I asked her to go back to a day when her Survivor Self was not present, a day when there was no pain, a day where she had fun and felt alive and free.

She shared a story from her early childhood when she was still living in her hometown in Turkey. She was spending a day with her grandmother, and she remembered cooking with her. They baked Caria's favorite cookies.

In that moment, she also realized how much she loved preparing her dad's meals for the week. She enjoyed putting it all together and surprising him with a new menu every week. He liked the food she made for him, but he worried that *it took her away from her more important job*, which was to teach those students in college. And he said he didn't care much about the menu if she didn't have the time.

Caria sat with this for a day or two and reflected on what she had learned in regard to her love for cooking. Soon her Survivor jumped in and laughed, saying that she was not going to do any cooking classes.

I said, "Why not?"

She said, "Well, it is not like I am going to become some kind of famous chef, now, is it?"

I responded, "Is this your Survivor speaking?"

She paused, smiled, and said, "I guess it is."

"Well, this is why we are not looking to wake up the Survivor and have it bring you back into the Waiting Room. We just want one class, one lesson, and one good cooking day for you. Can we plug into that, Caria?" I asked.

She said, "Yes, we can."

And Caria started a new chapter that day.

She always carried her Survivor with her, but she was able to talk back and act back too. And that is a big step out of the Waiting Room and making the Invisible Losses of her life less powerful and influential. She also remembered, through her Watcher self-visualization, that she was always creative and spontaneous as a young kid. But her time spent dillydallying next to her mom in the kitchen was never rewarded by her parents. So it never bloomed or was safeguarded. It got lost and held back.

But no more.

Coffee Break

I know you have questions. You may be wondering how you can ever forgive yourself for the choices you made in the past that you can no longer change. Also, how do you allow the kind of self-witnessing that needs to take place for healing without anyone else helping you with that witnessing? How do you make your Original Self mirror strong enough for self-reflection, for as long as you have to?

This is the part of the journey that you have always protected yourself from (Survivor), and it is why you can live a long life inside the Waiting Room, convinced that everything outside is way worse.

Self-inquiry is hard at this point in the process because when you step into your inner world, you start to question your current and seemingly self-reliant identity. The question *Who am I, really?* is thrown at you, and you would rather avoid it at all costs. This is where a lot of people want to go back to the Waiting Room, and you *can* go back to it, for a little bit of time—but not yet.

And you may be thinking, *What have I really accomplished so far with this book?*

Sure, you have gotten yourself to see that some of your life choices were made out of fear, even though at the time you thought you were making the best choices for yourself. *Great*, you may be thinking. *So what?* This first step has been so hard to take because it is much easier to stay with what we know works and believe the Survivor's lies about our past stories.

To question the past takes guts. To want to remember the wisdom is brave.

But you won't regret getting to know your Original Self and what your true story is really about. Now let's go and meet your Thriver. This self is quite the fun ride, which is why it has been hidden from you the most.

Revealing the Thriver

There is a part of us that gets eradicated early in our lives due to its unsustainable playful character that butts heads with the Survivor. This part is made of an untethered and free force that exists within us: it teaches us how to walk, to stumble and fall, and to quickly get back on our feet again. Which is the complete opposite to just surviving after each fall. It speaks to us words of excitement and living an unconfined life, thinking of play and boundless acts of amusement, regardless of a direct environmental conflict. But after a while, and as time goes on, Invisible Loss is deadly to the Thriver, and it eradicates every path toward it. It is almost impossible to thrive, to giggle like a kid again, when you have been hit with multiple Invisible Loss experiences that drained the life out of you. Anything that could offer you a moment's bliss is dangerous to the person who has endured unimaginably complex loss.

Therefore, we must learn how to thrive, a task that requires practice.

Thriving is the most underutilized and neglected part of our being. Not because we were not born with it but because the ordeal of surviving invalidated memories took its toll on us during our developmental years. We must figure out how to liberate the Thriver from the daily annihilation at the hands of the Survivor. After all, the Thriver is the Survivor's worst enemy. You can only imagine the ammunition that is sent out when it tries to emerge.

However, the Thriver is our escape from Invisible Loss, and once we find our way to the Thriver Self toward the end of the journey, it may feel sudden, even though it isn't. The Thriver Self will seem bigger than you could have imagined, larger than life. If it is a boat, think of a speedboat. If it could fly, it would be a rocket. It feels like this because the Thriver Self is the part of your Original Self that was here to have adventures and fun, almost childlike.

As you know by now, the Survivor Self is extremely protective, and its protective force won't release you, even for a second. You have to not just escape but become good at disappearing out of the Waiting Room for a thriving adventure, as the Survivor Self would chain you to the floor if it could.

Ways the Thriver Makes Itself Known

As we move forward, please take note of the list below, as it is critical to be able to detect when the Thriver is seeking to free itself from its Survivor-made cage. It can be difficult to spot the Thriver reemerging since it has been concealed for so long, and you may have entirely forgotten about that side of yourself. Take notes and keep an eye out for those unexpected Thriver visits in the coming days and weeks:

- Increased readiness to try new things: You may find yourself waking up on a Monday morning when normally you feel dread and your Survivor Self is at its best, but instead you have the urge to try a new coffee shop on your way to work. Or you consider a yoga class after work and reserve your spot right there and then. It could also present itself as saying yes to an invitation from a friend for a midweek hike, which you would normally never agree to. In other words, there is a stronger current to fight the Survivor voice when life is knocking on the door with something new.

- Seeking opportunities versus looking out for threats: There is a shift in how your thought process works when it comes to your outlook for the day. When your Thriver is engaged, you are interested in finding ways to enhance your life or career. In Survivor-based thinking, you would spend your energy on avoiding, deflecting, and defending whatever comes your way. Your Thriver, though, enjoys making the most of whatever time it has available. For example, you could easily find yourself saying yes to a block party where you get to meet all the neighbors from your street. This type of activity is something you would usually avoid like the plague, but this time you're eager to make a new friend or two. You end up laughing out loud a couple of times instead of judging people's comments (Survivor Self holding you back). Your opinion about these folks in your neighborhood changes from "They don't have anything in common with me" to "I think I may come out to this thing again next month and join them for weekly pickleball games."

- Decreased worry about doing enough, working enough, being good enough: There is a noticeable change in how you value or measure yourself when it comes to how much work you have done during your day. You measure the quality of your day based not on how much work you have accomplished but instead on whether you had fun and had a good day. For example, when you go with your daughter to the mall, you spend time thinking about how you want to hang out with her more instead of whether you have time to do it. There is no questioning that anymore. You do what feels good for yourself and the people in your life.

- Making concrete plans for play versus just thinking about it: The Thriver is a very action-oriented part of you. It doesn't just think about doing something fun; it does it. You know you are in your Thriver Self when you act on things you have wanted to do for a while. Or when you concretely plan future events that you've been postponing. It is about doing versus thinking about doing. The Thriver wants to play today, and it does that without being stopped by the obstacles the Survivor throws its way.

We will delve into the Thriver more when we step into the Integration phase of the Life Reentry journey, and you will feel more ready to confidently tap into your Thriver Self. For right now, think of these last few pages as an introduction to your Watcher and Thriver, nothing more.

....

Homework Prep: Processing the Introduction to the Three Selves

It may feel a little obscure to think of yourself as fragmented into three distinct parts, but it is going to make a lot more sense as you continue taking the first steps in your own Life Reentry. For now, this introductory glimpse is offered at this juncture to allow you to start looking at your whole life from a new place of understanding, in preparation for the Life Reentry process. But you must be gentle on yourself. Becoming aware of all these new touch points in your psyche can feel unsettling at first.

Even though we are still just getting started, you have already increased your self-awareness enough to no longer be who you have been—but you are still not who you will become. You are in the midst of change itself. You are reconnecting with the witness (Watcher) of your Original Self, and your dreams and wishes are starting to matter once again. When that happens, you begin your journey of reentry, remembering yourself but still in the darkness of the Survivor's shadow.

It will feel disorienting.

There is a lot of new information to consider. Right now, the only things we know how to do when something is coming in strong is to either run away from it or fight it. We do those things especially if it is challenging our safety and the life we have worked hard to make. Therefore, we begin gently, slowly acknowledging the new thoughts that are emerging. Acknowledging new or conflicting information is one way we can begin to process things in preparation for Life Reentry. Simply acknowledge in a few words how you feel about what you have read so far.

First Impressions
Write a few sentences on your phone, on your tablet, in your journal. For example, you can begin your journaling page with

- *I have felt a need to write down how I have been feeling and acknowledge . . .*

- *Even though I feel more confused about my past, I am starting to understand myself better, especially when I think about . . .*

- *I feel the need to be more honest with myself about . . .*

- *Lately I felt like . . .*

One-on-One Conversation
If you can do so, have a conversation with a trusted friend about your first impression of what Invisible Loss is and how it pertains to your life.

It's important that whatever enters your inner world is greeted, processed, and validated, because this needs to be done before you can begin to accept it or reject it as your truth. By taking a moment to practice the above prompts, you're allowing yourself the space to greet, process, and validate your experience. In the past, you have likely received information, someone else's beliefs, data, agreements, and realities, without much preparation and space to organize your emotional reaction.

When we carry unprocessed emotions in response to something we have learned, received, or been told, that new input can injure our internal world. That injury then becomes anxiety. The anxiety caused by that unprocessed information can become the reason we never leave the Waiting Room. And as we discussed earlier, when we remain in the Waiting Room, we can experience additional anxiety and feelings of depression.

Initially the discovery of your Invisible Losses needs to feel easy to do, so when you sit down to ponder what has not been recognized as a loss in your life, stay with it for only a few minutes. Additionally, as you are getting ready to spend a little time doing the following homework exercise, don't necessarily seek a place in your past where you are directly feeling grief. The grief of your past Invisible Loss is possibly gone, but your coping mechanism that was placed by your Survivor Self for you to survive that moment has created feelings of stuckness, anxiety, doubt, lack of self-worth, people-pleasing, or unhealthy boundaries. Look for those instead.

....

Homework: Trace Early Invisible Loss of Original Self

Now we will attempt to go all the way back to the beginning to track an early Primary Invisible Loss. Try not to feel the pressure of getting it right, even if you don't quite locate it here and it doesn't link to the Invisible Loss you tracked in your adulthood. You will have another opportunity in the next chapter to find it with a different exercise. These early exercises are here to give you a sense of what has impacted you and when before we step into the main part of the Life Reentry process where you will get clearer as to where your Primary Invisible Losses are situated. So let's start looking back to one of your first memories where you may have felt as if you did something wrong or you were scolded or reprimanded. Here are some questions to ask to trigger the memory:

- A recall of an early-age reprimand: Do you remember the first time a parent or a teacher told you off or reprimanded you in front of others? If yes, can you write down what you remember?

- Initial shift of self-perception: What did you think about yourself after the reprimand?

- Initial division of self versus the world: What did you think of those who reprimanded you?

- Initial feeling of shame: Did you hide your feelings about the reprimand from others? If yes, how did you conceal your tears or feelings of angst? Did you spend time away from others, isolating yourself in your room or outside? How did the hiding of your feelings manifest?

- Initial Waiting Room occupation: How did you process the shame, guilt, and anxiety on your own?

- Initial Survivor Self introduction: The Survivor Self is created by you as a child during the moments when you felt you had to hide your feelings of shame and grief. That is when you first gave birth to your Survivor Self. Do you remember an incident while interacting with friends online or in person when you said something to please them or fit in?

- Trace a new vantage point: When you go back to the memory, can you wonder something new about it? Something you have never wondered before. Imagine visiting this memory for the first time. What do you notice that you haven't noticed before? For example, was there something that felt unfair about your life when you were younger?

Now that you have completed the tracing of an early Invisible Loss, what surprised you about your new finding?

What would be a good description of this early Invisible Loss?

Chapter 3

Unlocking Your Story

M ost of us believe that we know our own life story well because we
have been the sole witness to that story from day one. Who better
to tell it than ourselves? But what if our own story was dictated by the
Survivor and not the Original Self? How can we be sure to find our way
to the intact memories of the Thriver and the accurate narrative of our
lives? Ultimately, your story needs to be told by the Watcher, recounting
Moments of Impact where you get to be a wise witness to what happened
to you in good and bad times.

In the introduction, you wrote down your Baseline Story. Then in
chapters 1 and 2, you spent time looking for Invisible Loss in your present and past. Now that you have early and current examples of Invisible
Loss, we are in a great position to map out your life's Waiting Rooms. As
you start to put the pieces together and glimpse the whole picture from
a wiser part of you, you'll start to unlock your story and become more
familiar with your Original Self.

The Importance of Sharing What Is Invisible

I am now going to share the part of me that has been the most hidden, and I look forward to you sharing your most hidden emotional self
afterward. Imagine if we always started to introduce ourselves with the
parts of us nobody can possibly know or guess. Trust would be plentiful.

Empathy too. But most of all, you would witness more people receiving validation. And because of that, there would be less suffering in our world and fewer invisible forms of loss.

You see, the decision to share parts of yourself with strangers is never just about you. It is an interactive experience between two people and their previously hidden stories. Once someone's story is seen, the other person's story begins the process of its own revealing and validation.

Of course, when you hand over an emotional experience that was born, lived out, and retired within you to other people in your life, you may feel like you lose ownership and control of it. Like it's no longer yours. But most of us recognize our own Invisible Losses only when someone else reveals theirs. And so, while I reveal the invisible moments of my life, you can notice some of yours. I hope at the end of this story, you get to share an Invisible Loss with someone in your life. The more you can share, the more will be revealed to you about your Original Self.

Template for Unlocking Your Invisible Loss

It took decades to untangle the complexity of a specific Invisible Loss of my very own and the myriad of Waiting Rooms that were obscurely sprinkled en route. We'll use the breakdown of my journey as a template for your own unlocking of your story. There are misleading turns along the way due to how the Survivor strives to keep us safe from more hurt. Adding this unlocking piece now will grant us access beyond the tracing of your Primary Invisible Losses. It will empower us to recognize the discreetly placed crossroads where your Survivor Self handpicked the direction toward a bulletproof Waiting Room versus your true aspirations or hunger for connection, creativity, and passion. Hence, you will begin to locate in your past your Survivor-influenced life exits and consequent Waiting Room entries. These junctions will be crucial to note in your journal, as they will be the accurate places for your points of Life Reentry.

This additional level of awareness you'll gain from the breakdown of your story will allow you to course-correct sooner and embark on your destined path. Trust that within your past, unbeknownst to you, there were experiences that belonged to your Original Self. These experiences were taken from you due to your Moments of Impact as their aftermath resulted in unforeseen circumstances, in people operating from their Survivor Selves toward your decisions, or in unforeseen events deriving from all of the above. As you read my life's Invisible Loss and Waiting Room entries, note any insights you are getting for your own story, as you will use this exact template below for your homework at the end of this chapter.

- The expression of desire: I was sixteen years old, living in Greece, and dreaming of becoming an artist. For as far back as I can remember, I wanted to be an artist. Everywhere I went as a young kid, I carried a pad and pencils with me.

- The Collective Survivor Voice: There is a Collective Survivor Voice that we must also battle alongside our very own. In my case, that Collective Survivor Voice stemming from most of my family members and friends was convinced that it was something I would grow out of, since most kids like to draw. And kids often talk about how much they love art. There seemed to be nothing special about my wanting to do art. *Why should anyone take it seriously and help me make it happen?* that Collective Survivor Voice said repeatedly.

- Hidden Original Self: However, deep down, I have always known (Original Self) that art was not only something I loved doing but also a part of who I was born to be. Without it, everything felt wrong. Even when I was much younger, my awareness of the significance of art was ever present. But it was squashed by the Survivor early on.

- Original Self attempt at true expression: When I was six years old, my mom took me with her to see a neighbor's art studio. I walked in and was in awe of what I saw in front of me. Paint tubes were scattered at this big table next to a palette that had all the colors of the rainbow. It was messy in there, but in a good way. I remember my mom telling the artist how I wanted to be a painter when

I grew up. I just stood there feeling glued to the floor, as if this studio belonged to me. As if I had been there before. As the years went by, I took art lessons at a couple of local places. I asked my parents if I could study art when I graduated from high school. They were hesitant because they wanted me to study something they believed could financially support me in the future, and they did not think art would quite do it (Collective Survivor Voice). We went back and forth for a while. When I finally convinced them that it would be the right thing for me to do, the high school told us that since we had missed the admission deadline, they would have to get a formal letter from the education department that would allow me to make the switch. They told us it was just a formality, as they had never had anyone not be able to make this kind of change. They were so sure it would not be an issue that they went ahead and switched me to art studies while they were waiting for the official response.

- Moment of Impact: A month went by, and life was finally feeling easier. For the first time, I loved heading to school in the morning. We started learning color theory and the foundation of skills for drawing. I have vivid memories of that month. It felt like my life had started to finally belong to me. I rested there. I let go of the other world I used to inhabit, one of traditional math and Greek literature and the nagging constant pressure to keep up with everyone else's choices. Unfortunately, when we finally heard back from the education department, our request had shockingly been denied. Now that I think back to that moment, it's strange that nobody tried to fight that decision, including me. At the time, my family and I simply accepted that I'd have to go back to what I had been doing before. I was devastated.

- Primary Invisible Loss: The next day, I went back to my old classroom, which happened to be across the hall from the art amphitheater. I spent the next two years watching art students go into that art class while I stayed outside. What I didn't understand for a long time was that my Invisible Loss of not being allowed to do something I craved, something that felt easy and right for me, influenced all the choices I made thereafter.

- Waiting Room life: I spent the next ten years working harder than ever to go to college in a foreign country and study in another language. Sure, I continued to draw and paint on my own, but that was no longer my priority. I put my creative side inside the Waiting Room and was told by my Survivor Self that art was not something I needed to do now. I even forgot that initial feeling of joy and freedom I had when I was temporarily moved to the art classes. I replaced them with continuous feelings of fear and dread.

- Survivor thoughts strengthening: I started to believe that art was just a fantasy for me. Something that could never be a real thing I could have for myself. I had to find a way to let it go and move on to something that I felt I could realistically (Waiting Room entry point) reach for. That was when my life took me on a completely unrelated path. One that was not bad per se but never felt quite natural or as creative as I needed it to be. Back then I didn't have the words to express this. I was living a good life, one I could be proud of, studying at a prestigious college in England. Making a good life for myself, just not being my creative Original Self. But what was really happening was that my brain was protecting me against fully living. I felt guilty if I did not work hard to succeed. I started to perceive my art as wasting time and taking me away from more "important" business.

  My Survivor Self rejected that original artist in me, scolded my fantasies about it, taught me to keep my head down and work hard no matter what it did to my physical health or my mindset. After all, according to my own Survivor as well as the Collective Survivor Voice, "life is not meant to be easy, not for me, and not for others like me." My family used to tell me when

I was growing up that my head was up in the clouds too often and that I'd better come down and face reality like everyone else. I finally gave up on those clouds and got myself down to earth, where I was expected to be. I started to believe that this was my only option, that in real life, people don't get to choose the kind of life they craved. The hunger for my art seemed to be unreasonable to all others and, in the end, to myself.

- Invisible Loss: This was an Invisible Loss of not being given the opportunity to choose a life for myself. Ultimately, I convinced myself (Survivor) that nobody really gets the choice to do exactly what they want. Fate is what is waiting for everyone. And my fate was not to go to school to study art, even though it felt (to my Original Self) my destiny. So I stopped pursuing it. After all, how can you pursue a life that you never thought could belong to you? Even when I fantasized about the life of the artist, I created a world of impossibility. I told myself I was not a good enough painter to succeed in this field (Survivor-based belief leading to the Waiting Room).

- Future catastrophizing: To protect myself from being disappointed again, my Survivor convinced me that I would have failed at it if I had tried, and so I stopped trying.

- Long-term Waiting Room residence: To survive my Invisible Loss of losing a life in painting, I went to the Waiting Room for a very long time. I made my permanent home in a place in *between* the life I had to leave behind and the life I could have had as an artist. In it, I built other rooms for my Survivor, who needed more space (getting stronger and taking up more of my thoughts) as time went by. I found myself succeeding in my other work. I'd even admit that some of the additional Waiting Rooms were enjoyable to reside in.

- False positive: A life in the Waiting Room doesn't have to be a bad life to be wrong. As a matter of fact, I'd say the majority of Waiting Rooms are made of good enough marriages, good enough jobs, good enough choices. In my Waiting Room, I experienced fulfillment in ways I'd never thought were possible. I became an author of books that have helped people cope with grief. And for a few years, I even believed that despite all the hardships of my life, I had managed to come out of my Waiting Rooms with my head held high. What I didn't know was that I had been inside a Waiting Room that my Survivor Self truly hid from me.

As you will see, the further we travel on this journey, the more the Invisible Loss that started it all ultimately becomes known to you, ready to be processed and healed, while at the same time, you finally respond differently to what happened in the past. You'll find then that your life begins anew once your reaction to your old story changes. I can't say it has been easy to find my way to a life as an artist, but I have finally gone back to school to study art—making that high school dream come true. The bliss that I felt is so much more powerful than what the Survivor Self could provide.

Your own personal Life Reentry may have nothing to do with art, but I know that whether you are in a wrong or good enough relationship, wrong or good enough career, wrong or good enough location—whatever it may be—it is worth your time to stay on this journey, identify your own Invisible Loss, and recognize the Waiting Room you hadn't noticed all along.

Now let's unlock your story and put it into the template I used above to make it easier to navigate your way through. But before we get to that, let's make sure you have time to process what you have just read and learned about the Original Self and how it gets hijacked from narrating your true life story.

Homework Prep: Processing Additional Waiting Room Entry Points

We are still in the Awareness phase and about to go deeper with how your story comes together from a new point of view. The Invisible Loss you discovered in the last chapter belongs to a bigger story arc. We will place it in the story, and we will seek to find its aftermath, its footprints on your life. Before we go to the homework part, let's process what you were introduced to in this chapter. You got a glimpse of what your Original Self may be like and how it has been kept invisible to you by the Survivor. Did you notice your Watcher Self reminding you of your Original Self as you were reading that section, or did you feel as if you had no access to that part of you? Either way, with this next homework assignment, you will get closer to unlocking the parts of your life that remain locked.

Homework: Unlock Your Waiting Room

In your previous homework, you glimpsed only your Invisible Loss and your Moments of Impact. Now let's try to spot at least one specific Waiting Room entry point to allow your Life Reentry to begin. Grab your journal and let's start putting your story into the unlocking template below.

- Start here: You can either use the Invisible Loss you have discovered from earlier chapters—and build the story before it and after it so you can see the whole arc—or use another point of entry (trace another Invisible Loss) into this unlocking process to reveal an additional Invisible Loss to yourself. Always remember, most of us have at least a couple of Primary Invisible Losses that are significant enough to keep us in long-term Waiting Rooms. Just start going through the template and see what pops up. Here we go.

- The expression of desire: Was there a time in your life when you expressed a desire or a need to your family, to your friends, or even to yourself?

    You can use these prompts to start your unlocking:

    - *I remember when I really enjoyed . . .*

    - *It is now clear to me that when I . . .*

    - *I loved hanging out with . . .*

    - *Whenever I sat down to . . . I felt such . . .*

- The Collective Survivor Voice: Do you remember an imaginary or non-imaginary pushback if you expressed your craving or need? Was there someone telling you that what you wanted was not possible? Did you have an inkling of what might happen if you did what you wanted to do for yourself?

- Hidden Original Self: If you felt this pushback, what did you internally know about your own self-expression—whether in life, work, creativity, or relationships—but not acknowledge or trust to be true?

- Original Self attempt at true expression: What did you attempt to express with your Original Self? This could have been a creative endeavor, like stepping on a small stage or writing something special. It could also have been you expressing your feelings to someone in your family or a good friend. A need to express yourself without restriction verbally or nonverbally.

- Moment of Impact: How did you get knocked down, and what was that first Moment of Impact? It could be the Invisible Loss you already discovered in the previous chapter or something else.

- Primary Invisible Loss: Share what you experienced after that Moment of Impact.

- Waiting Room life: How did your behavior and actions change from then on?

- Survivor thoughts strengthening: How did the Survivor Self convince you to stay in the Waiting Room?

- Invisible Loss: When did you stop pursuing your true expression of self?

- Future catastrophizing: To protect yourself from being disappointed again, how did the Survivor preview the future with you? Which future failure did it pinpoint so you would not want to try to give your Original Self expression a go?

- Long-term Waiting Room residence: How long have you been in this Waiting Room, and how has it evolved over time?

- False positive: What has been good enough in your life, and why have you stayed in this place?

II

Defensiveness Phase

Interrupting Survivor Thoughts with the Stack

*The truth is, the beginning we don't remember, the end we never see.
We die in the midst of running errands and pleasing other people.
One day we will just not be here, and if that doesn't motivate us,
I don't know what will.*

Defensiveness Phase
During this phase, you get to spend time listening in to
and interrupting your Survivor thoughts, cleansing them,
and ultimately reframing them with your Watcher.

Lesson
How to manually layer our thoughts, learning how to create a
Mental Stack that will be the gateway out of the Waiting Room.

Chapter 4

The Mental Stack

Cleanse, Pattern, Reframe

Congratulations for all the work you've done to get to this level of readiness. As you launch this next step in the upcoming days, you will use the knowledge you acquired about your Invisible Loss and its Waiting Rooms to help you during the challenging moments of this second phase. This upcoming step in the Life Reentry Model is what we will call Mental Stacking. This phase will conjure up some feelings of defensiveness as you courageously bring to light how the Survivor is influencing your daily thoughts. Due to this influence, the Survivor so far has been succeeding in holding you hostage in the Waiting Room. After the Awareness phase (the focus of the first three chapters) comes the Defensiveness phase (the focus of this chapter). In this phase, the Survivor persona will fight to stay in charge and keep the Waiting Room occupied to protect you from that Invisible Loss, which has multiplied to additional ones in your recent past and present.

This chapter is about shedding these life-robbing thoughts that have been occupying your mind and attempting, for the first time, to take back the controls. You could say this chapter is about seeding a new plant or writing a new code. To be able to do this, you will have to become attuned to what the Survivor thought patterns are. We will undertake this task here with this new practice of *Mental Stacking*. The Stack is made of the following:

- Writing your streaming thoughts
- Cleansing and reviewing them
- Spotting Survivor patterns of thinking
- Reframing them

You will be spending time listening in to and transcribing all your thoughts to first find that hidden Survivor pattern. The goal is to interrupt Survivor's repetitive fears and doubts. Once you do that, you can reframe these thoughts and make them ready for action. This is all-important, as it is necessary for the Survivor Self to fade into the background and for the Watcher and Thriver to take over the controls of your day-to-day life. If these first couple of paragraphs feel complex, please know that by the end of this chapter, they will make a lot more sense.

Keep in mind that reentering your life once is never going to be enough; it will need maintenance. Sweeping the floor one time won't keep it clean for the rest of your life. Brushing your teeth only here and there, when you feel like it, will keep you in the dentist's chair for hours on end. Not cleansing your Survivor thoughts will keep you in the Waiting Room or, worse, make you depressed.

The practice of Mental Stacking is one you will have to instill in your day-to-day routine if you want to interrupt the cycle of destruction that can be caused by Invisible Losses and that lands you inside the Waiting Room, keeping you an addict of survival. It's time to break free of that destructive cycle. But before we dive into that practice, let's take a deeper look at what this Defensiveness phase is all about.

The Defensiveness Phase

We start the Life Reentry journey having to fight a watchful but also oversensitive Survivor Self. During this time, the Survivor will most likely also step into a narcissistic type of behavior as it holds on to the lies it has been telling you to keep you from risking anything at all. Your long-term Waiting Room adaptation has you forgetting any feelings of freedom or liberation you may have had before you got here. This insulated existence has been lifesaving for you; it is no surprise that you feel defensive toward anyone (including yourself) trying to convince you that this life in the Waiting Room may not be good for you.

At this point in the Defensiveness phase, getting a warm breeze from outside the Waiting Room—for example, an invitation for an intimate relationship—can feel like a considerable threat, disrupting the life you have made for yourself. If you are sensing any hesitancy, it is reasonable to feel like this practice may not be right for you at this moment. After all, you have gone through so much, and you have figured things out for yourself. What on earth could you have missed? Why would you choose to follow the practice I offer here to cleanse yourself out of this Defensiveness phase?

Your Survivor Self might jump in here and console you by injecting thoughts like *You don't have blind spots* or *You don't have to do this next part of the work*. It is understandable if you still trust these Survivor thoughts—after all, we don't know each other. Who am I to you to tell you these things? The Survivor Self has been with you a lot longer.

It makes sense that you would feel protective of the life you have made for yourself. Know that your intentions were good, and your survival skills saved you. And that's something to be grateful for. But that was the past. Now is the time to ask what you might find from exiting the Waiting Room. Ask yourself, *Where can this lead? What if these possibilities are something to get excited about instead of something to fear?*

What Is Mental Stacking?

Mental Stacking is the ability to manually layer your thoughts to replace unconscious Survivor-based thinking with Watcher-based thinking in order for it to be converted by the Thriver to real-life action. This Stacking practice allows you to access your true and authentic self (Original Self) and give it back the controls of your life. Here is what a Stack looks like:

- The Cleanse: Transcribing the automatic, routinely based, unconscious thoughts.

- The Survivor Pattern: Subtracting the thoughts of fear and doubt from that first layer.

- The Watcher Reframe: Writing the consciously reframed thought layer in the Stack.

- The Plug-In: Translating the reframed thought into action (we will dive into this in the next chapter).

For now, we're focusing on the first three layers (the Cleanse, the Pattern, and the Reframe). Each of these layers (also known as Stacks) helps you shift the inner narrative away from the primitive survival mindset acquired in the Waiting Room. Each Stack assists you in leaving the Waiting Room while at the same time adding a layer of self-integration (Watcher and Thriver will start to merge) as we continue stacking in parallel to each chapter's homework. With daily repetition, we will get into the habit of stepping out of fear and into more risk-based Plug-Ins (an action that prompts an exit from the Waiting Room), rewiring the brain to exit its survival patterns.

We will then fall into more of a maintenance mode, which is Cleanse, Pattern, Reframe, Plug-In. This 4-Tiered Mental Stack will be introduced at the end of this chapter as a daily five-minute routine-based homework. This maintenance practice will strengthen the reemergence of the Thriver, cement the Reframes of the Watcher, and solidify the habit of the Life Reentry practice. It will also serve as a daily or weekly reset to avoid long-term occupancy of the Waiting Room as we regain control over our Survivor Self. All of the above steps may seem overwhelming in theory, but I promise you it is easier than it sounds. Without further ado, let's jump into it now, starting with the Cleanse.

The Cleanse (Mental Stack Layer 1)

The Cleanse is unfiltered writing of your thoughts as they come to you in a stream of consciousness. It will require a daily practice of writing what's on your mind for an organic and habitual stacking of the thoughts. To successfully incorporate it into your existing routine, it requires a sense of ease—creating a rewarding and fun practice—otherwise it won't stick. As you read though this explanation of this layer and those that follow, you are welcome to also perform the practice. The Mental Stack practice as homework will be summarized for you at the end of this chapter as well.

The Practical Tools

You will need to decide what type of journal you will be using to record your Stacks. You could use the same journal (digital or paper) you used to write your Invisible Losses and your Baseline Story. The most important thing here is to find a practical and convenient way to spend a few minutes a day doing your Stack homework. You might use the Notes app on your phone. You could also have a file open on your computer if you spend most of your day working in front of it. Of course, the traditional pen and paper work too, but not if it's an inconvenience to write that way. If you love using a paper journal, then use that so you will be motivated to write in it, as your Survivor will try to embed obstacles in everything, including your journal choice.

Survivor Gaslighting Prompts

Once you are about to start, the Survivor will have you doubting yourself on what to write down for this Cleanse. It will scare you with thoughts such as *What if someone finds your journal and reads it? You would not want that. You can't possibly think about writing this down.*

You are now being asked to do the work in an intense and time-consuming way.

The Survivor will say, *You don't have time. This here, whatever this is, is not for you. Plus, you tried this kind of thing before, and it didn't work, did it?*

Don't listen to that voice that wants to stop you from leaving the comfortable environment of the Waiting Room. It will pull out all the stops to get you to stay. It will gaslight you, manipulate you. This is when you realize that this has been an abusive relationship with no healthy boundaries and why you will have to sneak out often. The fact is that the Survivor Self has made your mind its whole house and has taken over all the rooms and called them Waiting Rooms, and you are suddenly trying to take them back.

Don't ever think this will happen without a fight—without the craziness of self-doubt and the relentless fear of the unknown. Survivor will try to take you down in more than one way, and you will need to be ready for it.

This is me getting you ready. This is me telling you that you have been under the spell of an emotional abuser that, at the same time, has been presenting itself as your savior.

Oh, the duality. The splitting of the truth. The back-and-forth between the good and the bad of what this voice really is: a narcissistic bully that is afraid of the new life your Watcher is convincing you to begin.

I dare you to break the spell.

Start the Mental Stack Here

In the next few pages, you will be guided through your first Stack with examples and prompts. If you are not sure about something, you will be given additional examples of Stacks so that by the time you do your Homework, you will feel more certain about what needs to be done. For now, open a blank page and start to write whatever is coming to mind as fast or as slowly as you need to. Don't examine what you are writing. Just let it come out. Don't question it. If you are writing it, it is there, inside your mind. Walk it out. Right now. Before you read more words.

Write yourself down. Just write.

Write all the crazy-sounding thoughts. The *ums*, the white noise in between thoughts. The words you don't know how to spell. The made-up words. The words you never knew were there. Remember how we talked about the missing language of Invisible Loss? This is where you will start naming, labeling, writing.

This is your first Cleanse, and you may feel like you are doing it wrong.

You are not.

Trust me; the only wrong way to do it is not to write it. Once you start, don't stop until you feel like there is not much more that wants out, for today at least.

Write exactly what you have on your mind right now. At this moment.

Ask yourself the truth about what's here. This might possibly be the first time you are completely honest with yourself.

But keep in mind this exercise is not about what happened in the past. What you missed. What you didn't know. The wrong choices. The regrets. It is only about them if they are being thought about *in this moment* as you are writing. So if you feel regretful in this moment about something that happened in the past, then that's totally fine, as this is what's running through your mind.

Whatever is here from your past, it is not in the past; it is in the present. Whatever is here at this moment is a part of the now, even if it happened a long time ago.

You'll want to know how it shows up. How it speaks to you. What it says. What it indicates. What is its language of choice? Where does the Survivor have the bigger voice?

For example, your Waiting Room may resemble a life of caregiving to others and never to yourself, because the original Invisible Loss had you feeling guilty about thinking of yourself due to being the oldest child.

You are afraid to change that, I know. That is a natural fear, and we prepare for it. You want to do this for the people in your life, but I am going to ask you to do it for yourself. For your Original Self.

You are ready, now, to honor the needs, the wishes, the losses, and the parts of you that have never had the privilege of the caregiving you have so generously given to others. Complain away. If something has been bothering you about a colleague but you just kept it inside, spell it out on paper. Talk about what upsets you about it. How it affects your everyday life. What scares you about it even. In other words, let what is here come to the page. No filter. No Survivor judgment regarding what needs to be written down and what doesn't.

If you are still wondering about what to write down, the Survivor thoughts are kind of sneaky and are casually narrated inside your mind as you are doing the dishes or getting ready to go to bed, not even paying attention to your own actions. Suddenly, for example, you are thinking about the conversation you had with your mom on the phone. The whole conversation is playing back as you are brushing your teeth. Your thoughts then move to the conversation you had about it with your husband. You told him how tired you were, having to talk to your mom about her medical insurance copays. You are thinking about how you haven't shared with her what is going on with you lately. How she doesn't even ask about how you are feeling. How she always just thinks about herself. How lonely it has been for you recently. How you have nobody to talk to. Write this down; cleanse it. It is the automatic, unconscious thinking that goes on in our heads that we need to find and write down.

The Cleanse Review

Now that it is written, read it back to yourself. Review what you've written and look for any parts that are being repeated. It could be the same thought appearing repeatedly. The same feeling. The same fear. The same doubt. Highlight it as you go through the muddy Cleanse. Underline it. Label it. A part of you knows what you should be looking for. Allow yourself to find it.

The Survivor Pattern (Mental Stack Layer 2)

This Survivor thought that we are looking for is being narrated a few hundred times throughout your day, but in a slightly different way each time. The theme is the same, but it may sound different. For example, you may feel like you won't do well at an upcoming job interview because you think you don't have the experience they may need. But you also think you won't be able to bake the birthday cake for your daughter to her liking because you have never tried this recipe before.

These two thoughts have the same theme. They belong to the same narrative. You are not certain about your skills. In other words, you don't think you can succeed in something you haven't done before.

Let's go back to the last example, when you spoke to your mom earlier today. She indicated that you don't know how to help her with the copay and that your brother is better at these things. Right here in the middle of nowhere, your Invisible Loss of always being unfairly compared to your brother strikes. Now you are recollecting the Survivor-based memory that links the present with biased proof from the past to make this factual. This pattern stemmed from your Invisible Loss that split your incredibly adequate and skilled sense of self from the inadequate self following the Invisible Loss event.

You are reminded that your brother always got better grades in school and your parents were always prouder of him. He was fearless about anything he did. You are now experiencing a cluster of memories based on the recall of the memories that support your need to protect yourself from more of the same feeling of inadequacy. These thoughts are preventing you from believing that you are good enough to try something new successfully. The Survivor is trying to protect you from more loss.

This pattern of Survivor-based thought sits right in front of the door that leads you out. It repeats in similar ways every day, depending on which Invisible Loss is being triggered and which Survivor thought pattern is required to protect you from going after something that can put you in the way of what happened in the past. You stop yourself from reaching toward your more-than-adequate sense of self, as you have been convinced that it doesn't exist and, therefore, you will experience more rejection if you head that way.

All of this is taking place without you even realizing that there is an agenda, a theme, an outside narrator in the seemingly very basic thoughts of your mind. This is exactly where you will dive in and extract these thoughts so you can discover the not-so-casual element of the Survivor.

Identifying the Survivor Thought Pattern

You can't easily separate yourself from the narrator in your mind that is telling you how you always fail by accessing memories out of context and often enough to cement these as the primary experience of your past. But this is what we will do with the Cleanse. We will separate these thoughts that are being used by the Survivor Self to make you afraid, doubt yourself, or create insecurity without you even being aware. As far as you can tell, you are just thinking about your day. But the truth is, a very toxic thought process is putting a very negative spin on your life, about yourself and the future life you get to live.

If you can't spot it at first, go back and read it again. Look for a feeling, a theme, a worry, a doubt. The feeling is almost an echo of the thought.

Doubts are never just thought about once. Worries have the same trait. The same repetitive nature. It is rare for thoughts not to be repeated in your mind unless it's a new thought, which is a rare occurrence. It is the way your brain works.

A new study found that we think 6,200 thoughts every day.[1] In my experience, in my years of doing this work, I've found that 80 percent of our thoughts in the Waiting Room are negative, and 90 percent of them are the same as the ones you had the day before. For the Cleanse you are about to do, we just want to discover one of the thousands of repetitive daily thoughts—one for each Cleanse you do. The one sentence. The one thought. The one thing you keep feeling repeatedly.

This is the Survivor narrative. The belief. The one thought that governs how you feel and how you decide what happens next in your life. We need to pull it out of your Cleanse to distinguish between the Original Self and the fragmented one.

Here are some examples to help you with that first homework Cleanse.

Short Cleanse Example 1

I am a failure, and I will never succeed at work. It feels like no matter what I do, nobody notices. I am so done with trying. What is the point of it anyway? No matter what I do, nothing ever changes. I must be dumb.

Survivor Pattern: I am a failure. I suck at everything.

Short Cleanse Example 2

I don't think my new boyfriend finds me that attractive. After all, why should he? I saw pics of his ex, and she is a stunner. I mean, she may even be a model. And here I am, with that big forehead of mine. The clumsy walk. My hair looks like crap no matter what I do. I don't know why I am even dating a younger man. Of course he is going to leave me for a younger version of me.

Survivor Pattern: I worry that I am not pretty enough, not young enough. Not enough for him. I am consumed with fear of him leaving me. I am spiraling.

The Watcher Reframe (Mental Stack Layer 3)

It takes a lot of confidence and belief in your Watcher Self to rewrite a Survivor-based thought. When you begin to rewrite a thought that you have spent years of your life thinking, it will certainly feel unnatural, even dishonest. But this process of reframing cannot be skipped. Your mission is to find the coping mechanism responsible for putting you in the Waiting Room and then remove it.

This is hard to do, as we rely on that mechanism to protect ourselves from life and from further loss.

The rewriting of our worries, insecurities, and fears has been hard for thousands of people, so let me reassure you that you are not the only one who may struggle with this.

Reframing Tips

Here are some tips to keep in mind as you're writing your courageous Reframes.

Reversal of Trend: You can try to write the opposite of your Pattern and stick to a reversal method, even if you don't believe what you are writing is true. You will write it against all odds. This is the easiest option, practically speaking, but it's the hardest to do because your Survivor Self will fight you to your core. A complete reversal example of the above short Cleanse and Survivor Pattern could be:

"I am a success. I am good at everything I try."

Watcher Reminder Reframe: Remind yourself of something someone who loved you told you about yourself.

"My grandfather used to tell me that I was the best at never giving up. I worked the hardest of all of his grandchildren. He was right. I will never give up trying, and therefore I will succeed."

Watcher Memory Reframe: This is where you bring up an example of a time in your life when you survived something hard or proved people wrong. Something that proves the Pattern wrong. Something that proves the Survivor Self is a liar.

"I remember the last time I felt like this was when I failed my exams twice and didn't stop trying until I passed with flying colors."

Reframe Templates: Here are some sentence starters to help you with the first few Reframes:

- *Even though I have struggled with . . .*
- *It is important to remind myself that . . .*
- *Life has been hard on me, but . . .*
- *It sounds like I will never make it through, but I know . . .*
- *I know I can't change what happened, but . . .*

The Reframe portion of the self-integration is critical, as it can rewrite both your past and your future. When you are shifting your mind toward a newfound perspective and understanding of an event, you see the past differently, and you mold the future intelligently. You also start to remember the Original Self. So don't miss out on that part of loving yourself.

Here are the two short Cleanses from above, followed by some additional examples, but this time with the Reframe part added.

Short Cleanse, Pattern, Reframe Example 1
I am a failure, and I will never succeed at work. It feels like no matter what I do, nobody notices. I am so done with trying. What is the point of it anyway? No matter what I do, nothing ever changes. I must be dumb.

Survivor Pattern: I am a failure. I suck at everything.

Watcher Reframe: Even though I have been beaten down, I know that someone will notice my work ethic and my potential.

Short Cleanse, Pattern, Reframe, Example 2
I don't think my new boyfriend finds me that attractive. After all, why should he? I saw pics of his ex, and she is a stunner. I mean, she may even

be a model. And here I am, with that big forehead of mine. The clumsy walk. My hair looks like crap no matter what I do. I don't know why I am even dating a younger man. Of course he is going to leave me for a younger version of me.

Survivor Pattern: I worry that I am not pretty enough, not young enough, not enough for him. I am consumed with fear of him leaving me. I am spiraling.

Watcher Reframe: I know better than to think that I care for a man who likes me only for my body. I know this is not true. If Paul doesn't find me attractive, then there are plenty of fish in the sea. It is time to release the low self-worth. I am beautiful inside and out.

Cleanse, Pattern, Reframe, Example 3

I feel forgotten by my friends. Nobody understands how I feel.

I tried to explain to my boss this morning why I was late, and he did not understand that I could not leave the house because my husband would not come out of the bathroom.

He doesn't get how worried I am every day. How scared I feel every morning.

Sometimes I wonder how long I have left at my job. I think they might just let me go and make up some kind of excuse that they are downsizing.

I gave them ten years of my life; they know it is not like me to be late.

But it falls on deaf ears when I try to explain it to them. My boss never really cared. Even when I had to have my own surgery, he didn't even ask how it went. He reminds me of my father; he is the exact same. I feel like I am a burden here. Like I always felt at home.

Survivor Pattern: I feel like nobody cares about me. I am also thinking of the worst-case scenario. I am catastrophizing. The loop of my thoughts tells me that if I make one small mistake, the whole world will come crashing down on me.

Watcher Reframe: Even though I am afraid of losing my job, I also know I always land on my feet. My mom used to always remind me that I figure things out no matter what. Even if the worst-case scenario did happen, which it probably won't, I will find my way to another job. I am really good at what I do. I have done it long enough.

Cleanse, Pattern, Reframe Example 4

Why is everyone leaving me? I am fed up with having to be the one always left behind. Why did you have to leave too? We were good, weren't we? A beautiful home. Great kids. And you just had to go and blow it all up. You lied and cheated. You made us all feel like we were not worthy of you. I should have known that you would always think you deserved better. I did everything for you, didn't I? You lied and lied. I mean, did you ever love me? Were you ever real? You robbed me of my youth. I lost the best years of my life to a cheat and a liar. Why wasn't I enough? You made promises and broke them. I am so furious. I am so mad at you. You destroyed everything. You broke us. Even though I loved you with my whole heart. You didn't want it, did you?

Survivor Pattern: I am never enough. I am scared that I cannot live without him.

Watcher Reframe: This was not your fault. You did all that you could to save your marriage. Don't ever let him, or anyone, take that away from you.

Cleanse, Pattern, Reframe, Example 5

Yesterday I lost my job, and I nearly threw up in the bathroom. I have been at this job for ten years. I know everyone is losing their jobs right now, but just because many more people are left without work, it doesn't make this any easier. They gave me the news at a meeting I was supposed to be at with my boss. I walked in, and instead of her being there on her own, there were two other people from HR alongside her. I knew it immediately. They showed me the documents of transition. They kept everything unemotional and professional, as if I hadn't given my whole life to them. It was as if I had never been there. I had planned to continue working there until retirement, which was just two years away. How can they get away with such a decision? They know I was counting down the days. They knew I was nearly there. But they didn't care, did they? They didn't care about what that would do to me. My life. I sat there wanting to scream at them and tell them how horrible this was. But I had no fight left in me. I just stared at the floor. As if I was hypnotized by the carpet. I still can't eat anything. I can't stop crying. I have no idea what I am going to do now. I am sixty-three years old. Nobody would have me now. I am old, discarded. I just don't want to live anymore. What is the point?

Survivor Pattern: I am so angry at how they discarded me. How could they not care about my life and the years I gave them? I feel unloved. I know it is unhealthy to think of it this way, as love is not a part of the job. We are professionals, after all. But that is the feeling I am getting, and I will go with it. I am unloved. I am discarded.

Watcher Reframe: I am proud of myself for not completely breaking down in that office. I was professional. I stayed calm. I will figure out what comes next. For now, I need to find comfort in what I know deep down, which is that I had an extraordinary career, and I will figure out what comes next when I am ready. And I look forward to some free time. I have longed for a beautiful garden for decades; maybe it's time to go buy some soil.

Cleanse, Pattern, Reframe, Example 6

Oh, I don't get this part at all. Cleanse what? My thoughts? How can I cleanse them if they belong to me? Where do I take them? This makes no sense. I am probably not doing this right. I don't even want to do it. If I am getting this right, this is about facing our worst fears? Looking at ourselves in the mirror and telling the truth? Do I really want this? Do I want to know? What is the point of knowing? Don't I already know?

Survivor Pattern: How can I find a pattern in one day? Maybe ask this again on day seven? I guess the feeling here is resistance. Confusion. I am confused. Maybe that is the trend of my life.

Watcher Reframe: I just have to trust. Trust the process, as they say.

Cleanse, Pattern, Reframe, Example 7

What is the point of even getting up to have another day feel the same shitty way? I have to face the truth of my life and remember over and over again that John is gone. Gone and gone. And never coming back. How in the world do you rewrite this? How do you face it? What is the point of this? Isn't life hard enough? Adding another layer of work to my day won't help a thing. I am mad at this process. I am mad at this book. I am mad that I am here. I want to run away from everything. Just walk out of my life for good. John would be laughing at me now. He would be shaking his head and laughing at the same time. He would find the humor in everything. Even this. I know it's early in the morning and there is no way to get myself to a better place when it is still so dark outside. I get up so early every day. I wish I could just sleep in, as I usually don't fall asleep until 2:00 a.m. My doctor said that I need sleeping pills and not to be afraid of them. I don't want the stupid pills. I have never taken any pills in my life, and I surely won't start now. I am so lonely.

Survivor Pattern: Life is hard, and I can't even sleep. I don't trust my doctor. I don't trust this will get better.

Watcher Reframe: I have always loved mornings; I know I will find my way back to loving them.

Coffee Break

I remember what it was like to see the Cleanse take place in a Life Reentry group setting for the first time. I remember asking the group to share their Cleanses with each other publicly. It was as if their hidden and repressed inner worlds were let out for the first time.

This 3-Tiered Mental Stack overrides the suppression. It brings out the inner Survivor narrator in all its glory and removes the shame and guilt you normally feel and that are why you don't normally express any of it.

After a while, you are not even aware of your own truth. The memory of that truth has been long forgotten. Since the brain does not favor thoughts that you don't often visit, they get abandoned. One day you don't even remember your likes and dislikes; you have unconsciously copied those liked by the collective (your social groups, family, or colleagues) and grandfathered them as yours. But when you witness a collective Cleanse, where there is an external witness for your inner thoughts, not only do you experience validation for what you are feeling, but your inner thoughts get reflected to you. You start to remember who you are, what you really like and dislike. It is better than therapy. It's a kind mirror appearing in front of you, showing you all the parts of Original Self that were left behind.

Of course, since the book is being read only by you, you and I are the only witnesses to what you are experiencing right now. But you have the best witness residing inside you. You know this by now: it is your Watcher helping you remember your every thought and memory. Let it join us in these next few pages so it can help you reframe what has been left unattended for as long as both of us can remember.

Mental Stacking Tips

As you prepare to dive into the Mental Stacking practice, let's look at some tips that you might find helpful. Keep these reminders handy if you find your Survivor's defensiveness building up. You may even copy this list to your journal or phone for easy access when you feel like the Survivor is taking over your newly reframed thoughts.

- Trust the process: Hold to the certainty that you are moving in the right direction. As you adjust your outer world to match the inner changes that come about from these practices, you may find that you are challenged by others on your new choices and habits. Be wary of doubters, and hold on to your positive new direction.

- Question the past: Question everything you wished for yourself during your Waiting Room timeline, as some of your past goals or dreams could have been dreamed by the Survivor. What you may want out of your life now most likely won't be the same as in the past. Dare to question even the most attractive and previously desirable dreams. The Survivor often hides there.

- Believe in your skills: You have abilities, skills, and gifts you have kept buried deep inside since you were a child. Once you start the reentry process, you will need to reveal them. When you think there is nothing special about you, remind yourself that this thought comes from a Survivor-based narrative and stems from an Invisible Loss. Thoughts like *You don't have anything to offer* or *You are not that special* are Survivor whispers from your coping mechanism; they are meant to avoid the possibility of more rejection or new loss.

- Watch the language: You will have to persevere and insist on using Watcher language to bring forth solutions to issues that once seemed to have no way to resolution. There are alternative ways to express the deeper, unresolved, and unprocessed parts of you that previously had no permission to be shared. Life Reentry will provide you with a language of new beginnings in your journey out of the Waiting Room. Your Watcher Self will birth solution-based language once you start to learn how to reframe.

- The fairy tale is real: Your own version of a happy place is real, and you deserve to get there however challenging it may seem. Write this new belief in your phone, journal, or notepad, and carry it with you if you can. Read it often as a reminder during the times you question whether you deserve a good life.

- No clinging: When it is time to let go of the old behaviors and routines, you might attempt to linger and hold on to some of the stuff that appears to have served you well. For example, the need to be liked by your boss and to agree with their statements so that you are chosen for that business trip or for the upcoming promotion. You may cling to your persona as an easygoing individual, as it appears to be an asset (Survivor thoughts) since everyone seems to like you at work. You are afraid to "tell it like it is" since your Survivor has convinced you that if you speak your mind, you will not be liked or chosen. When that happens, redirect your mind to the encounters you now crave instead. Don't give another thought to the experiences you required in your Waiting Room, like the feeling following verbal validation at work. This switch will take practice, but we have the tools to make it possible.

- Listen in: The answers will always be there and offered by the Watcher Self. Finally, you'll learn how to access them with the Mental Stacking practice. The Watcher has transcribed, recorded, and memorized every aspect of your identity that you may have forgotten. Trust in that.

- Slow down: Lastly, you must go slowly before you can go fast. There is no rush, even if it feels like there is. Being patient and doing the work, no matter how many extra days or even months you need to add to your practice, are required. What will make a difference is starting this journey with ease, consistency, and trust in yourself.

- Simplify: Put one thought on top of the other. Like building blocks.

- Be diligent: You have to be diligent and add the Mental Stacking homework to your daily routine. At first it might not seem like a realistic goal to write down your thoughts every single day. But let me ask you this. Do you shower most days? Do you brush your teeth? This is kind of the same thing, but instead of brushing your teeth or cleaning your house, you will be cleansing your mind from the habitual survival mechanism your brain has brought along after the Invisible Losses of your life. If we don't do that, the Waiting Room residency becomes permanent.

I know you can do this! Let's stack your way to a new life.

....

Homework: The 3-Tiered Mental Stack

As I mentioned in this chapter, each layer (the Cleanse, the Pattern, the Reframe) adds to a stack. The Mental Stack begins with a Cleanse, a Survivor Pattern discovery, and a Watcher Reframe, and later (chapter 5) I add Plug-Ins. Then the shift will start to be experienced just before rediscovery and reentry.

Schedule Setting

If you can find five minutes of flexible time in the morning, you will commit to cleansing and stacking then. If the middle of the day works best, then add it to your calendar as a regular meeting. Call it "Original Self Time." Or a word that signifies a sense of self. It could be the words "Truth Time" or "Life Reentry Time"—whatever label you choose is fine as long as you show up for that five-minute meeting. And, of course, you don't need to spend just five minutes. Fifteen minutes is even better, as you will really have time for a good Cleanse to allow more transparency into your mind. But five will do if that is all your Survivor Self will let you have.

Make sure you review your written words and find the doubt or fear thought. Then tap into your Watcher's wisdom and reframe it. Don't overthink this part; trust what comes to you. Open your journal, sit in a comfortable place, make sure you have a glass of water (or a cup of coffee or tea) next to you, and start to stream your thoughts. Use the Stack Template and prompts below and copy down the Stack just like this:

1. The Cleanse: Stream your thoughts, without any filtering or editing.

   - *Today I feel like . . .*

2. The Pattern: Spot the general feeling of the Cleanse. What is an emotion, a thought, a feeling that is being repeated?

   - *I am scared of . . .*
   - *I worry about . . .*
   - *I feel as if . . .*

3. The Reframe: Rewrite the Pattern with your Watcher's wisdom and memory of your Original Self

- *Even though I worry about . . .*

....

Homework: Rewarding the Stack

Once you finish each one of your Daily Stacks, it is crucial to reward your brain for working hard. Even though the experience of the Stack itself can feel good as you continue to make a habit of it, it is not enough. You will ultimately sense the freedom of reorganizing your day and being more in control of your inner and outer environments, but at first it won't be perceived this way; this is why you need to add a small reward at the end of each Stack. The reward induction during this juncture of the Life Reentry process will mimic an action-oriented step (a low-risk Plug-In) leading you out of the Waiting Room, which is always a threat to the Survivor persona. For example, choose something as simple as buying a new pen to write with, or treat yourself to a new coffee mug at the end of the first stack week.

Some people's Survivor thinking minimizes this added reward part, as they believe it's too simple or that they don't need it. Remember that it *is* needed, more than you know. You must connect the Stack to a reward experience for it to stick, since its premise is to reframe your Survivor thoughts. Also, the reward doesn't have to cost you money; it can be a reward of time to do something you have been feeling too busy (Survivor) to do. Giving yourself permission to watch a movie, even when you have other work to do, just because you have been Stacking is a rewiring experience. It basically teaches you that this process automatically gives you something to enjoy.

III

Action Phase

Exiting the Waiting Room by Adding Plug-Ins

*What you may wish for yourself now
is not the same as what you wished for yourself before.
Question everything you ever wanted.
Living fully is your birthright.*

Action Phase
Moving from the Defensiveness phase of internal processing
(Cleanse, Pattern, Reframe) to the Action stage of experiencing
(plugging in) and finally leaving the Waiting Room.

Lesson
How to use real-life action to step out of the Waiting
Room in a measurable and life-changing way.

Chapter 5

Escape from the Waiting Room

So far, we have managed to listen in to our thoughts, record those thoughts on paper, find our Survivor thought patterns, and then reframe them. Next, we will focus on that Reframe and make it actionable. We'll finally experience the work we have been preparing for. We are basically bringing the Life Reentry homework to life, and that means you are about to take your very first walk out of the Waiting Room.

We had to do all that stacking, Invisible Loss discovering, and starting a daily practice of cleansing, pattern finding, and reframing to get to here. It is late at night in the Waiting Room, the Survivor Self is finally asleep, and we use the Stack as the flashlight on our way out the door. Don't try to exit without it. Without the Stack, you may still find yourself out of the Waiting Room, but you won't be heading in the right direction.

For example, Mia, a classical violin player who has played the violin ever since she can remember, had some early success due to her talent and hard work, which didn't come easily. In her early childhood, her father enforced daily practice for her and her brother for hours every day. They could not hang out with their friends or even with each other until the very end of the week. Her Invisible Loss was that spontaneous playtime was discouraged, as her Original Self could play for hours with her brother out in the yard. She was often scolded by her father for "wasting time" outside. Mia grew up with a father whose Survivor Self convinced him that his children had to practice harder than all the other kids to be sure to "save" them from the same struggles he had faced.

Even though Mia is now in her forties and no longer lives with her father, she felt a lot of guilt if she said yes to a social invitation without having practiced on that day. Once she realized what her Invisible Loss was, she didn't even wait to do a Stack to decide on a Plug-In (action step). She went for what she thought logically was right. She decided to stop practicing the violin on weekdays and just practice on weekends. This change left her with more freedom during the week to be spontaneous. However, it soon created an added strain in her marriage, since she had less time to spend with her spouse. She also completely stopped her daily stacking, and she found herself back in the Waiting Room, putting aside her spontaneous Plug-Ins in order to preserve her relationship with her spouse. She told herself she didn't really need to be spontaneous after all. Mia didn't realize that this was really her Survivor trying to use the excuse of salvaging her marriage to stop her from being spontaneous and get her back in her Waiting Room.

There is tremendous power in identifying the Survivor—the fear-driven inner caretaker. The more we can recognize the Survivor-based persona, and the more we identify it in our Cleanses, the easier it will be to use Watcher and Thriver language to stack all the way to the Plug-In. Adding the layer of Plug-Ins to your Stack puts your escape from the Waiting Room into action.

Moving from a life made to protect you to a life created to *fulfill* you is a courageous act. This is why we must break down the process into intentional steps, so you don't have to be brave to become whole. You just have to keep reading.

I understand that changing your life feels overwhelming, but starting over doesn't have to be some big project. You just need to make a few simple choices without overthinking to start making your way out of the Waiting Room of loss.

At first, shifting out of Survivor thoughts could feel like a threat to your safety net. It may even seem as if you are being asked to jump off the train while the train is still in motion. It's the reason why taking one giant step doesn't work for most of us. It is why we stay in the Waiting Room longer. Why you will have to crawl your way out, looking like you are dillydallying—because if the Survivor notices even a subtle change of thought, it will attempt to scare you by reinforcing that old, internal misery you feel so that you stay put.

Because of this, we will take things slowly, so that we don't clue in the Survivor that change is being made. Think of this action-oriented part of the Life Reentry process as short escapades: you will be tiptoeing out of the Waiting Room without alarming the Survivor, who causes you anxiety and fear and ultimately keeps you from exiting.

The action that induces an exit from the Waiting Room is called a Plug-In. It is a kind of hookup. In many ways, you are hooking up with life. The action you take to exit a Waiting Room is generated by the Reframe you have been doing in the previous chapter. If you've been honest with yourself, the action you choose to take with this next layer of the Plug-In will induce a good feeling, which increases your dopamine, thus counteracting the fear response that's generated by your Survivor Self. In that positive space, life can be experienced differently for a few precious seconds, even minutes, giving us a glimpse of what it's like when we change the narrative by reframing the old story. Ultimately, you'll experience a shift to a new vantage point. Not only does this action need to be easy and right, but it should also be calming to your nervous system. You basically need to feel in control of your environment and your sense of safety while at the same time staying true to that Reframe.

Example of a Plug-In

Even though you will be exiting your old life, you don't want to be feeling as if you are too far away from what is familiar. Here is one example of what this might look like:

- Let's say that your Cleanse this morning mentioned how you worry about your kids always seeing you struggle and never upbeat.

- Your Pattern is that you always seem to worry about how you are being perceived by your kids, so you take steps based on what you think they need.

- Your Reframe reminded you of how you were always the friend who lifted everyone up and made those around you laugh.

- Your Plug-In could be hanging out with a friend on a school night, if your kids are teenagers, let's say. Instead of staying home and always taking care of them, you are looking out for *you* one evening a week. You start to worry less about how you come across to them and more about how you feel about yourself.

Whatever you choose, it should feel good, but it also must be slightly challenging, and that's a fine balance to strike. Your Survivor Self may tell you that you don't have time to watch a movie or see a friend. It is more than likely that your deadlines at work will be looming over you that day. You will have to push through your routine of survival to say yes to this simple but effective Plug-In.

At first, a Plug-In is a low-risk, high-yield return step. The first time you go through the Life Reentry process, or when you are reentering from a difficult period in your life, always start with the lowest-risk Plug-Ins.

The Importance of Starting Slowly

The Plug-Ins after Invisible Loss are small steps toward a feeling of freedom. They are simply paving stones that lay the path toward a renewed sense of being that was previously left behind. They are planned, controlled exposures to situations that typically provoke anxiety and fear. This slow progression is very important to the process. This is because you experience a form of cognitive distortion of the future, which is primarily led by the amygdala, a pea-sized part of your brain that is responsible for tracking your past anxiety-induced experiences. When it anticipates the occurrence of a negative event, based on what has taken place in the past, it suppresses your dopamine so you can't see the possible reward of that future event if you consider heading that way. In its effort to protect you, it stops you in your tracks on your way out of the Waiting Room by removing your ability to spot pleasure and reward and then basically removes your motivation to act on it.

When you start to plug in to that calming and controlled new experience, your brain is using a type of communication called an electrical impulse, creating a new pattern of neurons that "plug in" together for the first time. This hooks you up with a new thought for this new experience. This new thought can be something like *Well, this wasn't so bad, now, was it? Maybe I will do this again next week.*

Scientists call that the firing of neurons; I call it *Plug-Ins*. The more you plug in to these, the more you reinforce the new life, the new thought. But what you will be going against is a prolonged exposure to low dopamine due to the unprocessed long-term reaction to your Invisible Losses. This unfortunately guarantees a fear response the very moment you try to be brave (even a little) once again. The fear response will make varying attempts at sabotage each time you try to take a new type of action.

Your Survivor Self may obsessively be focusing, for example, on how these Plug-Ins affect the people in your life who depend on you for their own safety too, real or not. You may have many employees to care for. A big family that relies on your paycheck. A spouse or partner who can't live without your constant help; you worry they would not make it if you made any changes. Aging parents need your attention. Small kids need your good-night stories to go to sleep. Dare I say, ignore these worries for now; this is just what we call the *long-range catastrophizing* of the Survivor. It prevents you from thinking about change and is the reason we start small. Remember that big things can have humble beginnings.

No leaping for you and me—but plugging in? Yes.

Let me assure you, you *can* build a completely new life from the oldest and most entangled Waiting Rooms. But rebuilding and integrating your sense of self and wholeness is a complex and intricate act. How can you possibly get your fragmented selves to behave so that they can integrate and bring back your Original Self? In other words, how can you get away from seeing everything as an act of survival?

The Art of Designing Plug-Ins

You are going to have to arm wrestle your first precisely directed Plug-In. Your sense of freedom is not articulated and expressed easily, as it has been hijacked and hidden away for months, years, or, for some, even decades by the Survivor. Finding the Plug-In that can open the door, or even unlock some of the locks, may feel like the hardest experience, and it could feel like you are taking steps back.

This is exactly how it should feel. Being discouraged and feeling defeated are parts of the reentry experience. I have rarely seen this process happen without the back-and-forth or the frustration of the accidental wrong Plug-Ins. Or even the Plug-Ins that are right but backfire and produce a result that was not part of your intention. When you plug in and experience a glimpse of reentry, you may feel like you need to go back to the Waiting Room. Please know that this is okay.

This is going to be a journey, so you must remember that it may take some time to get your Plug-Ins stemming from your Watcher's reframe. Often you may find yourself plugging in with your Survivor Self, and you may not even notice it. This is part of the process, and the only way we learn is by trial and error. To find your way to the Plug-In that can truly help you exit your Waiting Room, here are some important guidelines.

Be Specific

First and foremost, Plug-Ins must be specific. The Survivor Self will try to convince you to do as little as possible or to not really do much at all. The Plug-In needs to be specific for you to feel accountable to yourself. For example, buying an outfit (easy Plug-In for a more difficult and bigger step later on) to wear to that holiday party (harder Plug-In) by the end of this week is specific enough. But don't just tell yourself to find something to wear for the party, as this directive won't motivate you to choose something new, something fitting your new life out of the Waiting Room, and something you can look forward to as a reward. This is so much more than just an outfit—it is your gentle unlocking of the Waiting Room door.

Make It Actionable

Your Plug-In must be something you can act on, not something you can just *think* about doing. There is a difference between an action-based Plug-In and merely the *thought* of a Plug-In. This may seem like common sense, but I have discovered that the Survivor mind plays tricks on us, and we think we have acted on something when all we really thought about was the *idea* of the act. So when you write the Plug-In down, just writing it is not enough for it to be realized. Or thinking it. Or wanting to do it. Or having the intention of doing it. You actually have to *do* it.

Make It Achievable

Your action has to be easily, realistically achievable. Planning something that entails a reliance on others, outside factors, or the weather, or even something that is impossible to get done due to circumstances, does not work. Your Plug-Ins must be easily executable.

Make It Timely

Be very clear as to when you will do the Plug-In. Time and place are crucial to holding yourself accountable.

The Plug-In Difficulty Scale

Finally, you will use the Plug-In Difficulty Scale to keep you within range so you won't activate your Survivor Self. It is easy to use, and it will keep your Plug-Ins more consistently doable and achievable.

Rating Your Difficulty Level

The scale goes from 0 to 10, with 0 being the easiest level and 10 being the most challenging. The scale has three difficulty levels: from 0 to 3 Easy Plug-In, 4 to 6 Moderate Plug-In, and 7 to 10 Challenging Plug-In.

How to Determine the Level for Each Plug-In:

- 0–3 Easy Plug-In: It is an easy Plug-In when the Survivor Self is not actively attempting to change your mind about it. You'll find yourself feeling excitement rather than fear, and you won't be tempted to delay or procrastinate. You'll be able to hear your Watcher's insights and beliefs with ease, as they won't be crowded by the Survivor as much. And even if they are, you will be able to easily reframe them and trust in the Plug-In's benefits to your life.

- **4–6 Moderate Plug-In:** It is a moderate Plug-In when you feel you are definitely stepping outside your comfort zone, yet it seems completely manageable. You are prepared for the challenge, as you can perform your Mental Stacking practice and feel stronger each time you contemplate the Plug-In and its consequences. The tools you are learning are designed to make the Plug-In not only appropriate for your life's trajectory but also achievable.

- **7–10 Challenging Plug-In:** This type of Plug-In will certainly feel hard, and you will doubt that you can pull through. That's why it should be considered only when you are at least a few weeks into your Life Reentry journey and your daily Mental Stacking practice has become a habit. When you step that far out of your comfort zone, Survivor's protection mechanism will undoubtedly get triggered. But if you're well prepared, you'll be able to push through your dread and reframe it for success.

How to Use the Scale

- At the start, stay in the 0 to 3 range. When you have a series of successful Plug-Ins (two or three will do), then move to the moderate level.

- Once you do a few of these successfully and maintain a Daily Stack practice for a while, you may feel ready to test the waters with a challenging Plug-In. If so, then by all means go for it.

- When you're ready, I recommend that you do one challenging Plug-In, then drop down to a moderate Plug-In for a few days, then go back to a challenging Plug-In.

Working Progressively

Here is an example of moving progressively along the Plug-In difficulty scale. Let's say you have struggled to keep healthy boundaries with your brother ever since you were kids. You always felt like your brother put you down in front of your friends when you were young, and now he does the same thing in front of your wife and your own kids. But he is the fun uncle, and your kids love him. You have been exploring your Invisible Loss of abandonment from your mom, who never stood up for you. When you got upset, she would tell you, *He didn't mean to say those things* or *You know your brother loves you.* Your brother would then tease you about going to your mom for help. You have been working on your Reframes, specifically to allow you to see yourself as worthy of attention and worthy of validation.

You decided your first Plug-In is to have a conversation with your wife where you share your feelings with her about your brother. Your wife has always been on your side, but because you have lost trust that anyone would care about this, you never really allowed yourself to be vulnerable with her. She also loves your brother and knows he has done a lot of great things for the family over the years. But one night, you decide to start out with an easy Plug-In and simply ask your wife a question about his behavior toward her. Nothing more than that. That question is received and results in a few minutes of conversation about her relationship with her brother-in-law.

The next evening, you plug in to that conversation, but now you bring up that you struggle with your brother's behavior toward you. You explain to your wife that it may seem subtle to everyone else, but the indirect comments about his job or his choices in life feel hurtful to you. This is a moderate Plug-In. Being vulnerable is something you avoid at all costs, even with your own wife. To your surprise, your wife's response is positive, and she is grateful that you chose to share this with her. Because of that, you continue to plug in moderately and share other vulnerable moments with her. You also plug in to other areas in your life with either easy or moderate Plug-Ins. After a few great weeks with successful Stacks, your Reframe takes you to a Plug-In that's going to be challenging. You now know you are ready to talk to your mom about this after all these years. This is a challenging, high-risk Plug-In. With your wife's support and trust in you, you feel confident enough to have that conversation. At this point, the outcome is not as important as the fact that you did this for your Original Self, who is someone who feels emotion strongly and needs to share it.

Supportive and Unsupportive Plug-In Types

Over the years, one of the main worries about the choice of Plug-In has been knowing the difference between a Plug-In that takes you *out* of the Waiting Room and one that keeps you *in* it. For this purpose, let's define those that are supportive and those that are not.

Life Reentry Plug-Ins (Plug-Ins That Take You out of the Waiting Room)

There are six different types of supportive Plug-Ins that you can choose from. They are Calming, Rewarding, Trusting, Bonding, Validating, and Loving. Getting a sense of these different categories will help you determine whether you're moving in the right direction.

- Calming: As I mentioned earlier, Plug-Ins need to be calming and nurturing at first. You need to feel good and at peace when you are plugging in the first few times. This is a requirement for the Survivor brain to not notice that you are attempting to change your life. For example, you may try fitting a short walk into your daily routine before you plug in to an intensive workout class.

- Rewarding: It must feel like a win, an experience to look forward to, at least at first. Without that, the Plug-Ins won't work, and you won't be able to continue your Life Reentry journey. You will need to think of smart and easy ways to immediately feel the reward of the Plug-In of choice. For example, add the reward of going to your favorite coffee shop. It needs to be fun and very easy to do.

- Trusting: The type of Plug-Ins that work build trust in yourself and in others. For example, by sharing something that is a bit vulnerable for you with a friend and trusting yourself to be OK about that choice.

- Bonding: The kind of Plug-In that helps you with intimacy, vulnerability, and connection with the people in your life. For example, spending time listening to your dad tell an old story about his time in the Navy. You'll find yourself more engaged with him and asking questions about that time.

- Validating: When you need validation in a choice you are trying to make, plug in to an experience that will help you feel more confident about a direction you are heading toward. Especially if you are drowning in Survivor doubts. For example, if you are trying to decide between going on a trip to visit your friend or staying home to finish a work project, choose a Plug-In that helps you move in the direction of your most feared choice, as it is likely the one that you need to move toward. Have a conversation with your colleague who can help give you a reality check as to how much time you really need for this project. Is postponing the trip necessary? Or are you just using the excuse of the project's deadline to avoid traveling outside your comfort zone? In other words, don't keep the fear inside; let it out, discuss it with the right people.

- Loving: Plug-Ins that help you experience a feeling of love. Spending more time with your dog playing on the floor and being silly could be just the right Plug-In, especially early in this process.

Survivor-Based Plug-In Types (Plug-Ins That Keep You in the Waiting Room)

Beware of these four unsupportive Survivor-based Plug-Ins—they are sneaky! They are Passive-Aggressive, Self-Depriving, Self-Protecting, and Recycling. They often disguise themselves as supportive Plug-Ins, but if you pay attention, you'll be able to see that you're working from Survivor-based fear. For example, you have known for a while that you need to be honest with your brother about the family home and that it needs to be sold soon to pay off debt. You want to be prepared for this conversation with your brother, so you start to do some research to find a Realtor to determine the right price for the house. Unfortunately, as you go online, you pick up a couple of home prices from the surrounding areas and call your brother with those numbers without diving deeper into the market. If you'd had more proof of the numbers—instead of a couple of superficial findings—the conversation regarding finding a Realtor would have gone more in your favor; negotiating next steps with your brother would have been easier. You reacted to something he said and rushed into it.

- Passive-Aggressive: You choose a Plug-In where, instead of speaking up in a difficult conversation, you stay quiet. In my classes, I often find that some participants will create a Plug-In that goes something like this: *Next time this happens, I will just not complain about it and be patient.* They believe (Survivor) that being quiet is the right Plug-In for them. However, this is a passive-aggressive Survivor-based Plug-In. A better Plug-In here would be using some of the wisdom from your Reframes to articulate your thoughts in a difficult conversation. Instead of not having the conversation at all (which is an unsupportive Plug-In), have the conversation in a way that honors your feelings regardless of what the response from others will be. Finding the courage to speak your truth even if you are worried that you will be misunderstood is critical in your journey of reentry.

- Self-Depriving: This type of unsupportive Survivor Plug-In is quite common. I see participants taking on weight loss in a way that is very self-depriving. For example, this kind of Plug-In focuses on your lack of something. They focus on severe discipline. For example, *I will not eat sugar and carbs this whole week*. Instead, you could plug in with *Today at dinner, I will choose those blueberries we have in the fridge instead of the cheesecake and see how I feel afterward. They seem as if they taste good. I've always liked blueberries.*

- Self-Protecting: Sometimes a Plug-In can seem right when we choose to not share our feelings with someone else, but often it is a Plug-In that is giving us permission to avoid vulnerability.

- Recycling: This is when you reuse an action that you completed at some point in your life in the past, for example, when you choose to plug in to something you have already done before. Going back to an old routine of, let's say, waking up half an hour earlier every day to read your favorite book. This Plug-In has no reason behind it. It is not connected to a Stack, an Invisible Loss, or a Reframe; as you know by now, your Stack and Reframes will ultimately lead you to a different Plug-In. The Survivor avoids new Plug-Ins by convincing us that an old Plug-In can work just fine.

Example of Joan's Unsupportive vs. Supportive Plug-Ins

Let me introduce you to Joan. Joan is struggling with her daughters being away with their father, having a good time without her. In her Cleanse, she talks about the fact that their dad initiated the divorce, but they don't know that he has lied to them in the past, and this keeps nagging at her. Joan wants to tell her kids that their father is not as great as they think he is. She questions her need to do that, but she also tells herself that it is not right that they don't know.

Here is an example from Joan's journal. She wrote this when trying to understand the difference between a Plug-In from her primitive brain and one from a higher-functioning place where the Watcher lives. Joan is going through a divorce after being married to her husband for twenty-five years. Her soon-to-be ex-husband is still very close to their three daughters, and they spend time away together for what Joan considers excessive "bonding" time.

MORNING CLEANSE: I woke up at least four times last night thinking about today's to-dos. Also ruminating about my conversation with my daughters. These questions and concerns kept running through my mind this morning. I woke up and it was clear that I want to tell my kids everything about their dad's shenanigans. They need to know all about who he really is, but I chose Plug-Ins without really paying attention to my Reframe. But once I wrote down the Plug-Ins, I kept finding my way to the shift that took place last week, where I realized that I need to learn to let go of control of everyone in this family. How this doesn't make me happy.

How can I tell my kids about their father without fracturing their relationship with him? I wish they knew who he really is. Lying to them too. I need to protect them from him. But he is their father.

PASSIVE-AGGRESSIVE PLUG-IN (UNSUPPORTIVE TYPE): Maybe just hint at what he is doing and don't go into the details. In this way, they know to look out for his lies so they can protect themselves.

TRUSTING PLUG-IN (SUPPORTIVE TYPE): Ask my children what they need to know about their father. Listen to their answers without jumping in.

Example of Designing Peter's Plug-In

Remember Peter's story from the introduction? He had been inhibiting himself from his nagging need to leave the Waiting Room since he survived his cancer. He wanted to move to a job that catered to his Original Self, which had wanted to step forward since his brush with mortality. His Original Self had been asking for a different pace and a new daily routine to follow, but Peter's Survivor Self kept pushing the Watcher thoughts and Thriver attempts away, forcing him to slowly go back to the familiar life he had before his diagnosis, making him even more entrenched in his Waiting Room.

After all, how could he abandon the place that had kept him alive? He couldn't see that the way he used to live his life was not as safe as he thought because the Survivor thought pattern circled around this worry. *What if I get sick again?* was a legitimate concern and a thought pattern that was not easily reframed. It continued to add more Survival-based thinking: *Who would be here to help me make it through financially if this happened again?*

This part was the toughest, as the arguments being offered by his Survivor Self were sound.

Peter thought about the risk involved (long-range Survivor catastrophizing) in going back to school part-time in order to work toward having his own private practice one day. And the further away he got from the dream, the faster the Survivor Self found its way back to his thoughts.

A perfect Plug-In for Peter is one where he can feel safe and calm about his decision to change his career in terms of his healthy prognosis and his financial freedom. How can Peter get all those things taken care of with one or two Plug-Ins?

Peter needs to strengthen his confidence in decision-making and to remind himself (Watcher) of his track record of always being responsible. Peter is now making space for a Plug-In that can guarantee him a sense of peace about his newfound eagerness for a more meaningful life. In creating his Plug-In, we look back to the Art of Designing Plug-Ins list that we covered earlier in this chapter (Specific, Actionable, Achievable, Timely) and plan for each of these items. We also look back to the supportive Life Reentry Plug-Ins list (Calming, Rewarding, Trusting, Bonding, Validating, Loving) and identify only those that are most fitting in this instance, as we won't have to have all items represented in each Plug-In when they are not all relevant. This is the result:

- Specific: Peter can plan a conversation with a good friend about this decision to go back to school—someone Peter trusts and someone who has known him a long time. In many ways, he is placing an additional Watcher Self (his friend) who can remind him of his own knowing of the truth.

- Actionable: This meeting with the friend needs to be set up and written in the calendar so it is something tangible. Peter must also make sure that he brings up his worries and his indecisiveness about his future career choice once he meets with his friend. Just meeting with him, of course, won't cut it.

- Achievable: This meeting is something that he can easily do. A short drive to meet his friend or a phone call.

- Timely: This meeting must happen in the next couple of days.

- Rewarding: It feels good to have a frank discussion with his friend, someone who respects him and knows him well. Being able to discuss his hopes and fears about this next career move feels like a relief, especially since he has spent so much time just thinking about the Survivor's "what-if's."

- Calming: The Plug-In also has to do with a sense of peace, as their meeting is at a restaurant he loves, a place where there's a serene atmosphere along with beautiful views. In general, location is important for the calming part of the Plug-In. Having this meeting at a close-by location where the noise level is high would not have been a good idea.

Redesign a Plug-In If It's Too Difficult for You

Even when we follow the template of designing the perfect Plug-In, sometimes it will feel like you are back in the Waiting Room even deeper than before. It's possible that the Plug-Ins are too difficult for you—they may be generating too much fear and triggering the Survivor. Consider asking yourself these questions to make sure you are choosing the right difficulty level. Low risk can mean different levels of difficulty to different people.

For example, how certain are you that you will achieve this Plug-In?

A Plug-In up to a 5 is a go, while anything over a 5 may need to be reconsidered: either make it more doable or change the Plug-In completely. Remember, it doesn't have to be hard to change your life for the better.

Joe's Story

Joe is nearly forty years old, and even though he has been leading a large international team and can speak in front of small crowds of his employees, attending unstructured social events makes him feel anxious. He will often isolate and leave early from any kind of social function where there is no specific schedule. This anxiety is felt even with people he knows well.

Since Joe's mother and sister are both alcoholics, he made the decision to totally quit alcohol about ten years ago. And he has successfully done that. However, since then, he has found no reason to go to restaurants or bars—as he won't drink, he doesn't see much point. Joe often mentions that he is not good with people and that he is short-tempered. He hasn't dated anyone seriously since his college girlfriend. When he is asked about that, he responds with a nervous laugh, making a joke that he is too hard to love.

Joe thinks his Invisible Loss is his dad leaving his mom for another woman and how Joe felt he had to stay with his mom most of the time. He is angry at his dad for leaving him and his mom, but in his daily Cleanses, he often mentions that his mom hasn't called him for six months and he is the one who always has to call. He makes sure to mention that when he calls her, she is always laughing about something silly, as if life is as it should be. His mom has remarried and is living overseas. In his Cleanse, he says things like, "It's OK for some," in reference to her living "the good life."

As he and I follow along his Cleanses, we notice his anger toward his mom a lot more than his dad, even though he mentioned early on that his dad is the one who left him. We start to see that the Invisible Loss is stemming from his mom, and possibly earlier, before his parents divorced. But for now, this is enough to go on so he can find his way to the Pattern, Reframe, and Plug-In.

His Survivor Pattern in his Cleanses shows passive anger toward his mom, as he often makes jokes about her life. Even though he is not angry with her directly, he has resentment toward her life choices. The thought loop that plays in his head is that his life is hard and hers is easy. He has to work a lot, while she doesn't do much. To him, living the way she does is irresponsible. His pattern of survival is to be responsible and work hard because if he doesn't, then he will be abandoned.

So he abandons everyone instead, especially when it comes to social and intimate situations. His Reframe here must be about letting go of his rigid schedule. Maybe even making an effort to interact with others. But of course, doing it in a way that's not too risky so as not to alarm his Survivor Self.

His Plug-In could be as simple as asking someone at a social event how they are doing—and staying long enough to hear the answer.

Joe immediately got to work on this Plug-In the very next day when he was meeting with some peers about a project. At the end of the meeting, he had planned a "small-Plug-In" that would allow for connection. He would simply ask a colleague about his kids. He believed he could do that, no problem. But once the moment arrived, he could not pull it off. He left as soon as the meeting ended. The Plug-In was more than just a small incremental step for Joe. In theory, it sounded easy enough, but in practice, it was too scary. Joe's Plug-In should have been easier, and maybe he could have sent the "small-talk" question in an email or a work text.

In Joe's example, a successfully redesigned Plug-In might look like this:

- Specific: Instead of making small talk at the end of a meeting, Joe will respond to an email and add a question about his colleague's son, since he had heard his colleague talk about his son being in the basketball finals at his high school. Joe will write out that sentence beforehand.

- Actionable: The Plug-In will be considered done when the email gets sent.

- Achievable: It is a low-risk Plug-In and easy to do because it is blended in with an email.

- Timely: He decides he'll send the email to his colleague by noon the next day. Not too late in the day and not too early.

- Calming: He could choose to send it from his phone while on his break. Or if it would be more calming just to send the email from his desk, then that would be right too.

- Bonding: When he gets a reply from his colleague, he considers a follow-up email of a couple of words responding to what his colleague said about the game, which would create a tiny bond, allowing for another question and a longer conversation.

Low-Risk and High-Risk Plug-Ins Both Have Value

While Joe may have had to initially redesign his Plug-Ins to simplify them, his work on Stacks eventually opened the door to a higher-risk Plug-In where he invited his colleagues to his house for dinner. The connection between Joe's relationship with his parents and the Plug-In of having people over for dinner is that for the first time since his college years, he allowed himself to let go of structure and responsibility and have fun with others, trusting that he wouldn't be abandoned the way he perceived his father had abandoned his mother (who, according to his Survivor memory, was having too much irresponsible fun).

Joe recognized that he had been protecting himself from additional hurt that could arise if he was careless with his responsibilities. He had to find reasons and ways to be OK with how things ended with his parents but at the same time work on building new relationships outside his job. That took him a while to get to, but he spent a few weeks working on his small-talk conversations and staying longer and longer at social gatherings. With time, he got to know his colleagues better, and the dinner Plug-In became less scary. He even said he was excited for everyone to enjoy his home. Joe was an antiques collector, and he secretly watched renovation shows all the time. His colleagues did not know this until they walked into his apartment. The dinner went well, and everyone gushed about his well-decorated space.

Additional Plug-Ins are becoming easier for him. His desire to have a partner in life is getting voiced more and more in his Cleanses and Reframes, even though the Survivor is busy telling him that he is "looking for trouble." Joe is reframing by focusing on memories of his dad loving him.

While progression to challenging Plug-Ins can be very valuable, it's also good to keep in mind that sometimes low-risk Plug-Ins can bring forth the most significant change because of the ease and calm they bring to your life. Rewarding yourself with these types of Plug-Ins can alter the course of your life in the most unexpected ways.

Coffee Break

Birds are *brave*. Not because they fly too high but because they fly *too close*.

Too close to our homes and us. Recently, I had so many birds get close to my windows. They fly, they stay for a few seconds, and then they *fly away*.

I realized that this is what courage may look like for birds. They step close to the edge for a few seconds and then return to comfort, which for them is the sky. I learned that courage looks very different for everyone.

For every single one of us, courage reflects the many pieces of our story. It is as unique as our DNA.

Courage for you today may look like simply walking outside to take a deep breath.

For someone else, courage is responding to a text from an old friend after years of silence. Courage could be putting on a dress you last wore at a dinner with the person you loved and lost. It could be playing the piano for the first time since you were a kid. Courage is not always a gigantic leap of faith but can be a quiet step toward the other side of your personal version of fear.

Being brave for you does not need to be compared with someone else's kind of brave. What is considered courageous to you could be a walk in the park for someone else. That should never make you think that you are not brave. You are brave when you choose to take a shower after days of not having the strength to do so. When you choose to respond to an email that has been waiting in your inbox for weeks. When you get up in the morning knowing it will be a hard day, and you get up regardless. When you look at an old photo even though it breaks your heart.

For someone who is in constant pain every day, courage may simply be opening your eyes and breathing and deciding to take another breath regardless of how difficult the first one was.

Courage sometimes is the ability to step inside your own pain and stand in it for three seconds before you step out. These three seconds make you brave. Don't forget that today, tomorrow, or any day after that.

Planning Your Plug-In

As you head into your own practice, here are some final tips to keep in mind:

- Don't overthink it: As you start to think about the first step you will want to make out of the Waiting Room, it is natural to overthink it. The Survivor voice will try to postpone the exit for as long as possible. It will make you doubt the choices you want to make. It will question it, even if it is a risk-free step.

- Take breaks: The bolder the Plug-In, the longer your return to the Waiting Room should be, at least in the beginning. You have to rest, cleanse, reframe, and slow it all down again before you go out for another Plug-In. It is important to know that this is a lifelong practice and not a fast and furious attempt to change your life. This is a way of being.

- Track opportunities, not threats: You are used to tracking Survivor threats day in and day out. Your thought process is normally trying to protect you from the cruelty of the world. For example, if someone is kind to you, you wonder what they want from you. You don't trust anything good coming your way. Under the guidance of the Survivor, you have become focused on dodging anything heading your direction instead of looking for life's opportunities. You may even think that everyone and everything is a threat, as your brain is used to thinking it is always under attack, as if the loss is still taking place. You will have to try to plug in to those instead of avoiding them like the plague. Intimacy. Honesty. Emotional transparency. These are not the Survivor's behavior traits. But they are human behavior traits.

- Don't make it goal-oriented: A Plug-In should never look like a goal but rather an expression of a love affair with yourself. It's a constant act of self-love. When you plug in to the expression of your Original Self, the Waiting Room walls disappear for a split second, but long enough for the mind to remember it.

Survivor Bias Alert

As soon as you start to plug in and you are spending more time away from the Waiting Room, you may notice that the Survivor will be attempting to remind you of things to worry about. There might be a sudden increase in anxiety in your Cleanses. Make sure you are spotting old and new Survivor patterns popping up, as a lot of the fears will not be as factually accurate as you may have thought.

You're now noticing the Survivor is quite the liar.

It can be hard to detect, as the Survivor part of our brain circuit can appear accurate and factual. But the memory it conjures to keep us from leaving is often inaccurate. According to Elizabeth F. Loftus, a professor at the University of California, Irvine, our memories don't exist in the form of a mental library.[1] They are not literal representations of past events. According to Loftus, they are reconstructed, not replayed. They are not fixed or set in stone. Now think about what that means for us and our Cleanses. When the Survivor Self is trying to convince you not to go out for dinner with that new date you have planned, it tries to sway you by reminding you of, let's say, a failed date with someone from years ago. But the memory of that date is not 100 percent accurate. It may be telling you that your date did not call you back for a second date and that you were deeply hurt. But the truth may be that even though he didn't call you again, you didn't seem to care that much.

The Survivor may be mixing memories together. The truth may be that you went on a dozen first dates, and only one of them was hurtful. But your Survivor tells you all your first dates are painful. Don't forget that the cure is to cleanse away. Reframe like your life depends on it. And plug in to a step closer to whatever your heart desires. You will be whole again. You will remember that not everything hurt you. And you can trust the timing of your Life Reentry once again.

Homework Stack Prep: The First Exit from the Waiting Room

Using one of the Stacks that you recorded in your homework from chapter 4, design your first low-risk, calm, and rewarding Plug-In. Use the design instructions from the beginning of this chapter under the heading "The Art of Designing Plug-Ins" (Specific, Actionable, Achievable, Timely) and the list of Life Reentry Plug-Ins that follows it (Calming, Rewarding, Trusting, Bonding, Validating, Loving). Make sure you follow the redesign process if you end up finding that where you started is high risk. You will need to make sure that your Plug-In is a low-risk action toward one of your Reframes that you want to act on. Choose one that you know you can do. You don't need to be courageous with this first Plug-In. Plenty of time for that later on.

Betty's Life Reentry Homework Stack

If you're having trouble with this practice, here is an example to get you started. Betty decided to take the Life Reentry class because she had been feeling stuck after she retired from her teaching career.

CLEANSE: During the last few weeks, and since my last day at the school, I have woken up around five a.m. with heart palpitations. Sometimes I feel like I am having a heart attack. I told my doctor about it, and she did an EKG, but nothing came of it. She said it is stress from the unknown and that she sees this kind of response with many of her patients after they retire. I feel so lonely and scared when these palpitations happen. I am afraid I am going to die, and nobody will know. I have felt OK here and there, and sometimes I even have a few hours where I am not feeling this horrible anxiety. When I went out of state to visit my friend, to change my routine, it felt like the right Plug-In, and it was, but the trip made me feel overwhelmed, as I had to be with people all the time, and that was hard. I hit my limit. I am tired and feel like a cold is coming on. Maybe it's COVID. I don't know what I was thinking, going up there during such times.

I am now behind on all my paperwork for my accountant. I am meeting with him first thing tomorrow, and I am just so upset with myself for not getting this done before I left for my trip. These Plug-Ins are so overwhelming for me. My retirement dreams are not coming true. I imagined myself traveling extensively all over the world. I certainly did not see myself as weak, overwhelmed, and scared. I feel like I lost my adventurous self. I used to never fear anything. I wish I had someone to tell this to, someone who knew me before and remembered me as this fun person who never stopped even for a breather.

PATTERN: Survivor took over, telling me that I should not have gone to see my friend; that is all I am hearing, over and over again. I need to slow down and not speed up after my retirement. I have to think about my health, plus I have nobody else to take care of me if something happens to me. I need to respect my limits. I am no longer young and healthy.

REFRAME: I made myself a cup of coffee and waited for that sunrise I can see from the upstairs bedroom. The Watcher likes that space, so I went there to reframe my crazy Survivor. I even felt better physically as I was drinking my coffee. I breathed a little better and remembered I need to take care of the paperwork.

I am fast when it comes to paperwork, and procrastination comes from Survivor trying to sabotage my new adventures. I started to feel more at ease and began formulating a Plug-In for the paperwork, finding a reward when completed, and a Plug-In for my yoga hour, which has been so important to me lately. My Reframe is I can be healthy and strong if I make sure I move my body and slow down my breathing. Everything is easier when I remember to take care of myself. Then the practical things only take a short amount of time.

PLUG-IN: After I finish my Plug-Ins, for my health and practical matters, I will go and visit my neighbor, who is funny and always makes me laugh. She reminds me of myself, before I had my breast cancer diagnosis and treatment five years ago. I need to plug in to people who make me laugh as often as possible.

Betty needed to take care of her Plug-Ins around health and paperwork so her mind could venture further out into experiences that provide a feeling of freedom. And as you noticed, once an initial Reframe takes place, additional ones happen automatically. The circuit of thought that is taking place due to the Reframe can pull in more Reframes.

Homework: The 4-Tiered Mental Stack

Now your Stack is getting taller. You will have to not only keep your Cleanses going, spot the Pattern in them, and reframe the heck out of them but also start taking specific action toward a new life. We won't start with setting goals or spelling out dreams. It is likely that those would stem from the Survivor and would not lead you to the new life you crave. Instead, this step is about bringing the Stack to life with the Plug-In, building habit and neural pathway circuits by moving from primitive to executive functioning.

When you cleanse something invisible and find the Survivor narrative and reframe it daily, you are able to keep yourself outside the Waiting Room and be in control of your inner narrative. Your day becomes more intentional and guided as you plug in from your own Watcher and Thriver narratives versus unconsciously operating through the Survivor.

Start or end your day by doing the 4-Tiered Mental Stack in your journal. This can take fifteen minutes or less. Of course, more is always good. Continue doing these daily:

1. The Cleanse
2. The Pattern
3. The Reframe
4. The Plug-In

IV

Divergent Phase

Shifting Through the Watcher Self

*It is not the loss you have to overcome
but how you command yourself through it.*

Divergent Phase
To be willing to be seen as the outcast, the troublemaker,
and the rebel and to let go of your hard-won safety nets.

Lesson
You will feel regret and be furious with yourself and
others as you discover who you are, what you really
lost, how much you sacrificed, and what was lost to you
because you freely gave that part of yourself away.

Chapter 6

The Fork in the Road

···

The sooner you start saying yes to the Original Self that's slowly reemerging, the more *at peace* you will feel in the long run. This next phase will feel rebellious, as it is finally time to inhibit the Survivor Self from relentlessly and unapologetically questioning the Watcher voice. It doesn't matter how lost you have been or even what you have endured. What matters now is what you will choose to do going forward. How long has it been since you looked out for yourself or since you listened to your own advice about what it is that you need? It's time to confront the Survivor voice and remove it from its place as your daily companion telling you, *You don't have a choice.* Something wonderful can happen when you give yourself permission to express your Original Self, the truest part of you.

In this chapter, I want to remind you that you are capable of living a really good life and at last finding your way back to the self that is whole. But to do that, we must go after reclaiming that old Thriver attitude we used to have. You will have to learn how to hustle the Survivor during the Divergent phase. Life Reentry rewards hustlers, daredevils, thrill seekers, and self-actualizers. When you arrive at this Life Reentry juncture, you can't be listening to the Survivor voice telling you to make choices based on what others want or expect from you. This may just be the hardest habit to break. Especially if, for example, your Waiting Room is made up of the fear of disappointing your family. We surprisingly hold on to what we have created, to average success and contentment, fearing that if we let it go, we will not be able to get back to that "good enough" status. We avoid the notion of starting from scratch at all costs. Even if where we are today is not a good place to be, we stay there. For a lot of us, it is easier to stay in something, approved by everyone else as acceptable and fitting in, than it is to begin again.

Let's also look at the fact that when you have spent your life giving to others and never asking for what you need for yourself, you realize that unless you announce that you need help (a courageous higher-risk Plug-In) nobody will offer it. Unless you grab a megaphone (Thriver fun Plug-In) and climb onto your kitchen table and yell, *Help me*, they won't hear it. They have been conditioned to believe that you don't need anybody's help. You can choose to uncondition them. You need help. You always have. You always will. Especially right now, as you are about to change some of the choices you made in your life; you are allowed to change your mind about your own life's direction. After all, you are not here to please your parents, your relatives, or your friends. Let's unlearn that you are.

But the term *people-pleasing* does not clearly define the painful walk that takes place in between your Waiting Room and your life. It does not showcase the sacrifice. When the first intention is to please someone else, because you feel guilt or you have misplaced compassion, in many ways you delete the Original Self further. People-pleasing blinds others to your existence, and it is why they may now be reacting to your choices that you have newly based on your Original Self. Surviving your life required people-pleasing, saying yes when you wanted to say no. For instance, agreeing to go on a business trip when you didn't feel well enough to do so. You felt the pressure to get on that plane while not quite feeling like yourself. You wanted to not make a fuss, so you just kept going against your own physical and mental well-being. Your Survivor even convinced you that you would be just fine. You felt better a couple of days in, but you hated every minute of it. Getting on video with the client instead of chatting in person would have been good enough. You didn't need to bend over backward for this.

Speaking up about these seemingly small things you sacrificed will help you speak up about the bigger things you have given up on. Invisible Loss is a shadow that spreads over everything: your Watcher Self is revealing the shadow; your Thriver Self is ready to have fun with all the things you missed out on; but it is your divergency that will make you a whole person again.

Your Plug-Ins are starting to help you spend more time outside the Waiting Room. This next level requires a courageous advancement that—if not achieved due to its challenging higher-risk Plug-Ins—could derail the first few steps you have taken on your way out of the Waiting Room. Especially if you have yet to hold on to the new routines you have started to implement with your Daily Stacks.

The Shift

This part of your journey is the heart of Life Reentry, where the shift really happens. The divergent personality makes itself known at this stage of the process. It's a natural part of the Life Reentry continuum, yet it's messy, and it will stir up its fair share of trouble. At this point, you must come face-to-face with the years of self-sacrifice. You carried the heavy bags of others even though they were not always meant to be carried by you. You did it so you could have a better chance at belonging. You had to survive the world that was around you, and you did it the best way you knew how.

During this Divergent phase, you will make plenty of mistakes. The person you are becoming will feel imperfect. You will feel regret and be furious with yourself and others as you discover what you really lost, how much you sacrificed, and what was lost to you because you freely gave that part of yourself away. This process does not come without pain, as you will see yourself going back and forth between the new life and your life in the Waiting Room. It's like dating two people at the same time. You feel you are betraying both. You stay with the old life because you still have an attachment to it, and you know it really well. Yet you also step into the new with insecurity and doubt, afraid to jump in with both feet.

The Temporary Divergent Self

As the new Plug-Ins have become more routine for you, they're encouraging new long-standing habits. For example, perhaps you started to speak up during your weekly back-and-forth conversations with a friend instead of staying quiet. They may not like what you have to say, but you see that their response was not as bad as you imagined. Or instead, you realize their reaction to your sharing was not what you want in your future, and you are now contemplating whether this friendship is something you need in your life. Either way, you are entering a new chapter for yourself where you show up in your truth. When you continue to speak your mind, you start to create a repetitive activity, and it now becomes something that your brain no longer must choose. You will just see yourself speaking up, telling it like it is, and fighting for the things you want out of your relationships without consciously choosing those actions.

This chapter is about this *transitional period of chaos* as your two lives (Waiting Room life, newly discovered life) are passing each other. In other words, you must kick out the Survivor Self so you can use the services of your brain for new habits. It is indeed about becoming the driver of your car, but you must hijack it first. It's why you also seem different to others, but it's all about getting yourself back. You're getting back the part of you that was always meant to be yours.

This phase is the most uncertain you will be during the Life Reentry process, but it is also closer to the breakthrough moment you have been waiting for all along. Learning to trust this phase will help you resist the temptation to quit. And believe me, you will be tempted! You're starting to become someone you either can't recall ever having been before (loss of Original Self at a really young age) or someone you had to leave behind many years ago in order to avoid pain and hurt. Your awareness of what has taken place, the happiness you missed out on, turns your Survivor Self into an angry beast. And you'll be running away from it, making new mistakes, saying the wrong things.

In the early years of Life Reentry teaching, I only noticed the heroic element of this phase. I could not see the Survivor becoming aggressive as one leaves the new life behind. This period of divergence—between the Survivor becoming more aggressive and the external world of friends questioning your choices—will make things look worse than they really are. It is hard when some people in your life are not rejoicing with you in your celebration of this new chapter. Unfortunately and fortunately, some friends will come along, but others will not. Your Survivor will try to protect you from that by begging you to stop this *crazy talk*. But don't let it convince you.

Your family and friends might need some reassurance from you as you are plugging in to life experiences that surprise them. They are watching you withdraw from events you used to attend to religiously. For example, you never missed Sunday dinner at Grandma's house, but now you choose your own personal commitments to attend to, and you can't make it to Grandma's every week. You are spending your time and money in ways they may not approve of. You are traveling more often. Your routine is different.

At the same time, you are working hard at getting further and further out of the Waiting Room for a longer walk, convincing your family and friends to come along with you, as you need people around you to witness your journey. I hear the reassurances you have to give or the possible goodbyes you have to say. I see how much you want them by your side. It has been hard lately.

The Willingness to Stay in Reentry Mode

As I mentioned above, the first time you arrive here, you'll experience what it feels like to rebel against expectations. You are certainly willing, and you know this is the direction you want your life to go, but your initial interaction with this world of possibilities also brings forth more Invisible Losses. You are here and eager, but there is only so much you can process, only so much you are willing to see.

Remember, you need only be willing to look at one Invisible Loss at a time; the others take care of themselves. Once one of the most important Invisible Losses gets unraveled, it is enough to get you to a place of resources and support.

This part of Life Reentry will introduce you to a whole other way of living your life. For the first time, you will consider the possibility that you can take risks that will lead to a rewarding life. What if that's true? What if during this stage, while staying longer out of the Waiting Room, you get to mingle and interact with people who have found their way to a life that is created by choice and not by a reaction to loss and fear? These kinds of people love their jobs, relationships, and choices, and it shows in the way they carry themselves in conversation. They are honest in their responses, not trying to impress. Present while at dinner with you and not checking their phones all the time. Eager to take risks for what they crave by going after their own version of Plug-Ins that risk what they have already gained. But it is no longer hard to do, as plugging in at a challenging level can be easy when you practice and make stacking a part of your routine. It is the willingness to stay longer out of the Waiting Room by stacking and honoring the Plug-Ins by bringing them to life.

The Stack you are creating every day, as part of your homework, holds the key to a Plug-In that truly feels right for you, challenging or not. Each person's Plug-In is unique because everyone's Cleanse, Survivor Pattern, Reframe, and Watcher are incomparable, and individually tailored Plug-Ins are necessary.

You will be comparing every moment of your new chapter to the life you left behind. Your brain is used to processing the old data to understand your everyday reality, and it's doing it to also understand the new incoming story. Your new origin story.

The ideas, images, thoughts, and beliefs you have today (even after the Divergent phase) belong to a life that is no longer fully present. You may still live in the same house, be married to the same person, have the same job—but *you* are different. The shift you just experienced within you will slowly adjust the external look and feel of your life with time, but right now it can be disorienting to the new identity that is trying to flourish. The automatic comparisons are happening via the Survivor Self. It is comparing how things used to be with how things are every waking moment. It happens automatically.

The Survivor Self is looking to find familiarity in an unfamiliar new life. When it can't find it, it rejects it as wrong. But remember, new is not wrong; the new is not to be compared with the old. It is to be welcomed, stroked, and smiled at. The new cannot be seen through the lens of the old life. It would be like wearing reading glasses that don't magnify.

Coffee Break

Did you know that your heart might break, even when you are trying to do the right thing by changing your life?

When you change jobs, move towns, shift your ways of life for the better, you are more likely to be rejected and mistreated by the people closest to you.

It won't make any sense.

You are fixing some things, but other things are literally breaking.

The things that break are the things you thought would never break, so you hold on to them while you are positively changing your life.

When those things and people break, and they're no longer your unconditional foundation, you may initially end up in a worse place than when you started.

But whatever fundamental part of your life is being destroyed, know that it could not handle your new beginning.

It was never meant to be a part of it.

It was not supposed to come along.

I know.

It is hard to imagine certain people, or parts of your past life, not making it into your new chapter. You are feeling like your stomach is up against your chest.

You didn't see this coming. You really didn't.

But you couldn't have. You were a different person in the life you are walking out of.

That self could only see the view from inside that life.

As you started to disassemble it so you could travel to your next destination, your view was rearranged. You started to see things you missed before.

The hard thing to understand is that what you are seeing now is not new; you just could not see it before.

But it will still break your heart as if it is a brand-new loss.

You will cry about it. You must.

Then you will have to let go.

So you can make it to your new destination. As someone told me once, *Do whatever you have to do to get yourself through.*

The Higher-Risk Plug-In

We have now arrived at a place where you are starting to have the courage, the motivation, the newly found need to risk more. The good news is that the farther away you travel from the Waiting Room, the more the Thriver Self may be leading this journey. The power of the Watcher and Thriver selves working together can derail the Survivor Self, at least temporarily. The Survivor is currently attempting to persuade you to *quit this insanity before you get more hurt.* Did you know that when your brain is trying to stop you from anticipated danger, the suggestion of that danger makes you feel as if the danger is real, and therefore you feel fear? The same goes for pain. This has a name: it's called the *nocebo effect.* Basically, the suggestion of pain is enough for you to feel that you are in pain. You will think that this hurt you are feeling may be real, so expect it. Prepare for it. Cleanse it. You are cleansing your grief of the old life, and you are questioning if the fear and pain you are experiencing now are just an anticipation or the real thing. You are bravely trying to interrupt the old mindset and Survivor-based habits of your Waiting Room.

This next step requires a higher-risk Plug-In so you can keep staying out of the Waiting Room longer to allow the shifts that are starting to take place. This time out of the Waiting Room gets you closer and closer to the Thriver persona, and that is why the Divergent self is stepping in to make sure you get there. The higher-risk Plug-In needs to be planned within the 4-Tiered Mental Stack so it is targeted toward the expression of the Original Self versus the Survivor Self.

Maria's Story

Maria came to class a few years ago wanting to find her way to a new career. For most people who have had a lot of Invisible Loss, their need for change sounds much the same as Maria's.

She had started to feel physically unwell. She had no partner and no prior marriage or kids, but she had invested herself in building a respectable career as a doctor, where she had finally gotten the kind of professional advancement she had always wanted.

In the past couple of years, Maria had experienced a tremendous amount of anxiety on Sunday evenings as she was getting ready for the week. She was an organized and detail-oriented person. She had experienced direct and indirect bullying in grade school. She had to find a way to protect herself from more loss.

She noticed that being a really great student gave her some advantages and allowed her to be protected by some of the teachers who were witnesses to the kind of bullying she experienced. At home, she found that her parents didn't trust that she was telling them the truth about the bullying, even though she attempted to explain it multiple times. And she was not the kind of kid who kept things in to begin with. She was outspoken about what was taking place at school—but at some point, she gave up trying to convince her parents that, for instance, nobody sat next to her at lunch and that she was always accused of doing things she had never done. Maria stopped trusting her parents, and her way of surviving at school was to study hard to impress her teachers.

It worked.

Not only did Maria find a way to connect and be validated by her teachers, but she was also accepted by her peers when she was chosen for school plays, concerts, and spelling competitions. Not everyone, of course, liked this version of her, but she got enough attention and "love" to keep her going.

But as the years went by, Maria always felt that nobody really liked her for herself, and she felt that if it weren't for her achievements and accolades, she would have had no friends and people would finally know her real self, which, according to her, was not worth knowing.

Because of these feelings, all her career choices were derived from the need to be accepted and seen. She had been running away from rejection all her life, but the price she had to pay was a job she hated—something she never had admitted to anyone, not even to herself. How could she?

She was not even able to understand that her life was built on the need to protect herself.

That was when she came to my class.

Maria had finally gotten herself to a place where she could not do it anymore, and with the help of her classmates, she plugged in to a life she started to like. She found people who didn't pay attention to her profession or her achievements. These friendships started with a new hobby, and she made a couple of connections based on that interest. Maria loved interior design and loved watching shows about flipping homes. And because of her detail-oriented, note-taking nature, she created all these folders, files, and archives of tips and tools for the most cost-effective home renovation.

One of her Plug-Ins was to reach out to someone she met on a dating site. She went on a quick coffee date, but nothing came of it. During that coffee date, the other person mentioned to her that he was a part of a Facebook group with folks who flip houses on the side. She did a quick search, and without much trying, she found the group and joined it.

That night she spent hours reading old posts about how people got started. Maria had saved some money and decided to see if she could redesign the home that she had owned for ten years and possibly sell it. She told herself she would do it just for fun.

At this point, Maria had cleansed daily, with lengthy posts in the group. She was able to bring in many Reframes and see her Patterns loud and clear. She got to the place where she knew that underneath it all was her drive for achievement, and it made sense to her why she was in the Waiting Room and feeling the ways she felt.

When this part happens, there is always a sense of euphoria. Finally, we have figured things out. Seeing her Invisible Losses one by one and the trajectory of her life through the eyes of her Watcher gave her a lot of clarity. The part-time hobby Plug-In was not impossibly challenging. The Survivor gave her some hard times, questioning her use of time, doubting her choice, telling her that people in her circle in college would laugh at her.

It was the typical kind of Survivor attempt to keep Maria locked up. It didn't work.

Maria spent every weekend and evening working on her house. She even hired a handyman to help her with the bigger things. She realized she had developed a comprehensive step-by-step guide for how to do a small remodel. When she shared some of her before-and-after pictures in the group, a lot of the members were interested in her design tips.

The Sunday-night anxiety got worse as time went by, and it was obvious that it came from having to step away from her newfound hobby and go back to her career responsibilities.

She knew she had to find a way out, but how? This seemed almost impossible. Yet this job that she once prized was becoming her biggest dread. Her Survivor Self would tell her that if she didn't refocus, she would lose the respect she had garnered from her peers. She started having nightmares, and depression was setting in.

Her first Life Reentry experience now was the cause of her depression. She was starting to be mad at herself for starting this. Why did she have to mess up the best thing in her life? Her job was the one thing she could rely on. What was she thinking?

But what Maria did not understand then was that her saying yes to her true self, the part of her that may seem strange or problematic to others, was the first time she acknowledged who she was. It was the first time she allowed her true nature to be shown without fear of being rejected. And lastly, it was the first time she was accepted for who she was, away from the medical world.

She was standing right where you are. Having left the Waiting Room for short walks, she noticed that on one of the walks, the Plug-Ins lasted longer. This set of Plug-Ins brought a deep sense of joy—something that she had never experienced before, or a joy that she had forgotten.

Maria was thriving in parts of her life now and barely surviving in others. The contrast was causing more problems than before. But this kind of contrast is required for what needs to take place next. The divergent self can only exist in a rebellious state. Once it is there for a while, that rebellious self helps you reenter a life that, once lived long enough, feels truly in harmony with who you really are. The fragments of self can then come together to make the whole. And only the whole self can remain in a more permanent state of reentry.

Maria used the tools of Life Reentry and stacked her way through her hardest days. She cleansed and reframed. And soon she got herself to a place where she could resign from her job.

She did it in the same way she did everything else, with attention to detail, taking into consideration all the many parts of this journey she was about to end in order to begin her new life. She executed every part of it with the elements of the Watcher, who helped her create enough grounding to slow the process of her resignation without it being so painful that she rushed through it. She even inspired someone in her practice to start the reentry process herself.

Maria sold her house, and with the extra money she made, she started taking on clients who wanted to do the same thing with their own homes. Maria did not put together a business plan, and she did not plan further ahead than the first couple of months. She had learned that every week in this new chapter would give her so many shifts that she could not possibly plan too far ahead. Plus, she didn't need to anymore. She was enjoying her life. She was working hard, yes, but she had chosen this hardship. She even won a few competitions and made some extra money to allow her to purchase a vacation rental to renovate.

Maria's life was as she wanted it to be.

Of course, Maria's example doesn't show you the sticky parts that nearly had her quit the class and go back to the way things were.

Imagine changing all the parts of your life that are wrong for you. The chaos can feel catastrophic. It's important to keep in mind that trying to change direction, even at the smallest variable Plug-In level, even at the lowest risk, creates this turbulence. But even when you are influencing the direction of your life in an orderly and seemingly stable fashion, there is a good chance it will bring disorder into your relationships and work. A tiny Plug-In could tip over your entire life.

It could be one conversation you have with your boss about your desire to oversee a project. You are thinking it is a 5 percent risk, but you have never been someone who spoke of such things. You never considered saying out loud that you want to take on more responsibilities. But that unexpected moment at the end of a video call when you tell your boss you want to be a part of a project could change everything. It could give your boss an idea to move you out of state or even out of the country for a project you didn't even think was that big of a deal. You were just plugging in. Doing your Life Reentry homework. And just like that, the Plug-In shifted and put you outside the Waiting Room longer than expected, and it has you wanting to run back to it.

Imagine that this project requires you to move to a country you have never been to. Let's say you find yourself in Costa Rica or Norway, working full-time, making new friends. One small shift in how you saw yourself, which allowed you to tell your boss what you really wanted, may lead to your sitting in an apartment in a foreign place, scared to death but possibly open to this new feeling. A feeling you never had before. A small Plug-In can open the doors to ten new ones you didn't even initiate. I know this can feel scary, and this is where the Survivor Self will try to butt in, but now you are prepared for that.

You do a quick Stack:

CLEANSE: I shouldn't have gone for this. What a mistake I made. I wish I could turn it back to how things were before. Why did I mess with all the good stuff I already had in place? I feel sick to my stomach even just thinking about it.

PATTERN: I feel anxiety about future events that are completely unfamiliar, and I stop myself from taking initiative.

REFRAME: It is your choice whether you take that job in a foreign country; you are in control, and right now you are here, at home, with nothing to worry about.

PLUG-IN: Ask some questions about the move and find out more about it. Maybe reach out to your colleague who did the same move last year. Whatever you do, make sure you plug in slowly, gently, and with all the tools you have at your disposal from chapter 5 on designing your Plug-In and working with the 4-Tiered Mental Stack.

And just like that, you can prevent yourself from being locked in the Waiting Room again.

Following the Divergent Path

You are finally entering a passageway that shows you a new life. The Mental Stack you have been doing becomes the counsel you have always needed to gently guide you, where Plug-Ins become paving stones, revealing the hidden way to your reentry.

Where the Thriver dwells in innocence, wanting to play and have fun; the Watcher dwells in timelessness, always there to remind you of your truth; and now finally the Survivor is in waiting. The waiting has finally moved to the Survivor Self. It is the part that stays in that darn Waiting Room.

All of these pieces come together to bring you to your Original Self.

As you can imagine, having to take all that chaotic energy, contain it, and ground it in the center of self can mimic a tsunami, but we will do everything we can to minimize the chaos as you forge ahead. Remember, the chaos is temporary as you remove some of the protective elements of your life. The Survivor tries to hijack you by telling you there is no time for rebellious acts. Your Watcher steps in.

Time. There is no time in this part of the journey.

Stop the clocks. Hide the watches.

You shift your focus to today. True Life Reentry places you in the present state, without running out for a better glimpse of the future or ruminating on the past as a time that was happier. It is more like a feeling, a state of being. You are shifting out of both the past and the future, seeking to understand, process, and engage in *today*.

How does that look? Let me show you.

- You are never on a diet; instead, you eat for hunger.

- You don't take jobs for a future sense of security.

- You don't believe in an old, Survivor-based narrative, such as *No pain, no gain*.

- You trust in the unfolding of your choices.

- You live a life that never begs for escape; instead, it craves more work because it brings you life.

Yes, there are practical parts of living that need some planning, and you will have to organize some of the structure around the life you are building, but ultimately, your day-to-day decisions will be based on what is true for you and craved by you. The clock of this kind of life always tells you the same time. At this moment, it beckons for a longer day.

When this type of living is possible, Waiting Rooms are short-lived and easily unlocked. The loop of the Survivor becomes less frequent and easier to spot and reframe. Reframing is no longer a forced way to bring forth the Watcher. Your whole inner and outer worlds are reframed foundationally.

Yes, there is a way to live a completely different life. But you have to remove the Survivor's assumptions, as it will try to tell you, *It is not possible, and even if it were, it would not be for you.* But this life is not for the Survivor Self, and that's why it is trying so hard to hold on.

....

Homework Intermediate Stack Prep: Watcher Day

During this step, we are starting to see the shift that is taking place, and we must capture it so the brain can repeat it with ease. Can you write about your day, as you would in your Cleanse, but from your Watcher Self's perspective? You will have to talk about everything from that wise self, from the unworried part of you. Write for as long as you can. Stay with the Watcher voice almost as if you were writing a long Reframe. This step is going to help you make the Reframes more natural, and it will also help you shift to a more rational and logical perspective of your daily life. Here are some prompts to help you write this from the Watcher.

- *Today started with a sense of peace, especially when I started to think about . . .*

- *Work today was not so bad, even when . . .*

- *I felt ready for . . .*
- *I am starting to feel almost as if . . .*

Homework Intermediate Stack: Watcher Cleanse

You can, of course, still do your Cleanse with the Survivor thoughts as you normally would and reframe the pattern you see (basic 4-Tiered Mental Stack) or you can move on to the intermediate Stack, in which you cleanse from the Watcher if you feel strong enough to do so. If your Cleanse is from your Watcher, your Reframe happens automatically—in other words, you have reframed already; it is no longer the Survivor voice that is speaking. As stated in the homework preparation section, you begin your Cleanse with the Watcher voice. Use some of the suggestions listed above as well. Since you have transitioned from a Survivor narrative Cleanse to a Watcher narrative Cleanse, you then choose the next Plug-In, which is a higher-level and riskier Plug-In for you. The intermediate Stack consists of just two tiers:

WATCHER CLEANSE EXAMPLE: Work felt good today. It wasn't perfect, but it was good enough that I felt less stressed and more inspired. I even called my mom for a few minutes in the middle of the day. It turned out to be a good choice. She didn't look as tired as she usually does, and she even thanked me for calling her. Maybe I don't have to plan to talk to her every Saturday. I can now be a little more casual and call her during a break at work. She seemed to like it, and I didn't mind it myself.

PLUG-IN EXAMPLE: Now that I don't have to call my mom in the middle of my Saturday, I can use that time to go to the local modern art museum that opened last year but I haven't been to yet. It feels great to have a Saturday all to myself.

V

Integration Phase

Recalling the Thriver Self and Reclaiming
Your Original Self

Let go of the things that defined you.

Integration Phase
Integrating the three selves (Survivor, Watcher,
and Thriver) to reclaim the Original Self.

Lesson
You are rewriting the parts of your story, the parts where you
lost your playful self, specifically the part that was lost to
the Survivor narrative. You must grieve the realization that
you could have lived an alternative life if you had known the
truth you are observing and grasping about yourself now.

Chapter 7

Coming Home to Yourself

....

This last step is dedicated to the rediscovery of your Thriver, which will lead to reclaiming your Original Self, the part of you without the conditioning of the Survivor. This is you coming back home after having been gone for quite some time. We are now moving from the defensive mechanism of the Survivor to the open and playful state of the Thriver. We'll endeavor to activate it in the same way we activated the Watcher, by substituting Thriver behavior for Survivor behavior.

The Thriver is the persona closest to play and to the uninhibited expression of thought. We will attempt to get back some of the Thriver memories from an earlier time. These were eliminated by the Survivor, as it had to keep us safe from remembering how fun it was outside the Waiting Room. And if you can't remember how you thrived in the early part of your life, you can create Thriver memories from scratch. These memories will reconnect you to the relationship of the self that thrived. Because of that initial Thriver disconnection, you no longer have access to direct communication with the self that knew how to have fun and play. Instead, as you know by now, you were dialoguing with your fear response, which was blocking you from interacting with the Thriver in order to self-protect. That's why the Stack is a fundamental part of your daily journey: by controlling the narrative to include the Thriver and Watcher, you are able to get back your lost sense of self and become the true writer of the story of your life.

You are rewriting the parts of your story where you lost your playful self, the part that was lost to the Survivor narrative. For too long now, you have interpreted the events of your life through the filter of fear and survival, even when you were having fun. Once the events of your life were put through this filter, its narrative was witnessed through suffering rather than thriving. You could be out at dinner with your best friend, but you may be experiencing that event or retelling the memory of that event either as flat or with a gloomy perspective. This is a result of living through the Survivor lens, constantly distancing yourself from the Thriver.

Now that we are at this step, you will start noticing how routinely implementing Mental Stacking is steering you back to dialoguing with the Original Self. This crucial conversation allows you to discover that life outside the Waiting Room is not as menacing as you previously thought. Your brain is now finally making new connections, and these new connections are opening new frontiers for you. Through the understanding of your Invisible Losses, Reframes, and Plug-Ins, your Cleanses are starting to change from the Survivor writing them to your Watcher stepping in earlier in the Stack. It can now start the conversation instead of having to wait for the Reframe prompt.

This shift will be part of the admirable redemption of your Original Self.

Your Invisible Loss had you reacting to your life's perceived threats as though they were true threats, never allowing you to wonder if that perception was accurate. It's almost as if you were living in an underground bunker, and you're just now crawling out. The rediscovery of the outside world is both a tragedy and a resurrection of self. You must grieve the realization that you could have lived an alternative life if you had known the truth you are observing and grasping about yourself now. The good news is that after you do experience this initial grief over the lost time, you will continue stepping into the discovery of the path that belonged to you but was simply dormant, patiently waiting for your arrival all along. We will keep eliminating all the obstacles along the way to safeguard your journey there, so let's make sure you can successfully identify the Thriver and Watcher, because the Survivor can become very good at sneaking into the conversation without your noticing, reminding you of your past Invisible Losses.

Distinguishing Between the Voices of All Three Selves

At this point in the process, you will start to be able to identify the whisperer in your ear. Is it the Survivor, the Watcher, or the Thriver talking? The Watcher is always the witness and the reframer between the Survivor and the Thriver. The Watcher is also your witness of your sense of Original Self. When the sense of that self goes out of awareness, the witness within you is still there but not actively rewriting, reorganizing, and of course narrating the story of your one precious life.[1] You are in charge of activating that skill of the Watcher.

You now also recognize how crucial an updated inner narrative is in accessing the part of your brain that plans and reasons. Without that updated narrative, the old Survivor thoughts can still automatically escort you back to a Waiting Room mindset. As long as you keep the daily practice going, you will be getting closer to removing the limit on your capacity to begin again. Maybe even reversing some of the damage your brain endured as it "degraded" its higher functions for that long-term Waiting Room life it had to endure.

But as you come to this place, be aware that your Survivor thinking is not absent; it's just not as loud and prominent. Your Thriver and Watcher are starting to overpower the Survivor. As you proceed along the way, you will get better at distinguishing between the voices of all three selves (Survivor, Watcher, Thriver) so you can guarantee that you are choosing the right one to allow for that integration and recapturing of the Original Self. Here is the key to knowing the difference. Use these three cues when you are struggling to distinguish between them:

- When we listen to the voice of the Survivor, *we feel relieved* (because Survivor keeps us safe).

- When we listen to the voice of the Watcher, *we feel wise and loved*.

- When we listen to the voice of the Thriver, *we feel fulfilled*.

Ask yourself; are you relieved or are you fulfilled? Do you feel love or attachment? Do you feel wise or in doubt? Keep this in mind as you move forward in your journey of integrating your Original Self. The following is a practice you can try for distinguishing between those voices.

Homework: Conversation of Selves Stack

When you need to decide on something in your life and you can't make up your mind, do this Conversation Stack. Pay attention to what it says. It works fast, and it also gives us the truth about a situation where we're in conflict. Here is the template for this short but very solution-oriented exercise that can be done on the spot. Ask a question and try to guess what answer each persona will give:

- The Survivor always instills doubt and fear by saying . . .
- The Watcher always reminds you of your wisdom by answering . . .
- The Thriver always wants to act by . . .
- The Plug-in always brings the Original Self back to life by . . .

Here is a simplified example of the Conversation Stack in action. This example is about a relationship that may need to end, and you can't make up your mind whether it should:

SURVIVOR: You can't possibly consider breaking off this relationship. Stop exaggerating and being so dramatic. What happened is not as bad as you make it sound. Where will you find someone new to care for you? If you leave, you will end up alone. Just stop the dramatics and accept the apology. This incident won't even matter in the future.

WATCHER: This felt wrong, didn't it? How often did something feel this wrong in your life? You have only experienced two or three moments like this one, ever. This seems like a new fork in the road is waiting for you. Something has just ended. Let it end. Let her go.

THRIVER: It's about time. I am glad this happened. Send that text, make the call, and let's take a different path. Who knows what awaits you? I bet it's going to be fun. I can't wait to see what comes next.

PLUG-IN: Make a call and end the relationship. If a call is too challenging, send a text. You choose how to end this. Stay the Thriver course. It's over.

Now that you can Conversation Stack your way through difficult decisions—especially when you have some doubt—let's explore further how you can start to tune in to your Thriver without too much effort, since the Thriver has a prime role in the Conversation Stack.

Recalling Your Thriver Memories

It is not that you don't laugh in your current life or make new memories, but it may be harder for you to lose yourself there. You have forgotten the magic of remembering the details of a regular day. The routine of seeming nothingness. The luxury. The walks. The new friends on a summer's day while hanging out by the ocean. I wish you didn't need to go back to the past to get a taste of your Thriver Self, but Thriver memories don't just lie around, waiting to be remembered. If you have experienced a number of Invisible Losses, you will struggle to remember the carefree days of your life. I've learned, over the course of teaching Life Reentry, that when a person had to adapt and survive for years, or even decades, their thriving memories became obsolete.

Almost as if they never took place.

I can share with you many different examples of people telling me that they could not remember a time when they simply just had fun. They had convinced themselves that they were never happy, even as a young, carefree three- or four-year-old. Their memories of Invisible Losses may be positioned earlier than when they first happened.

Your Survivor-based brain will do everything it can to get you to the memory that reminds you how to act in order to avoid new pain, new loss, new sorrow. As you know by now, what is important for the Survivor is to keep you safe.

We are all made in a way that our survival is always the primary focus, and because of that, we'll always be resistant to any memory that tells us we live in a good and safe world. As a result, Thriver patterns have been left behind, without any tending to. We're usually not asked to remember the good times or to talk about the good stuff. There is so much focus on the difficult memories when we are courageously attempting to put the pieces of our lives together. It is essential to spend time remembering the act of thriving as a young kid or young adult. According to neuroscientists, we must spend time actively recalling our past experiences in order to comprehend the present from the perspective of the Watcher. Purdue University psychologist Jeffrey Karpicke says, "Every time a memory is retrieved, that memory becomes more accessible in the future."[2] The ability to revisit the right memory is crucial to how your brain will also build your future. And as Trevor English puts it, "When you build memory, you're essentially telling your brain's electrician to lay some new wiring up there. When you remember something, it's like flipping the light switch and seeing the wiring work as designed— the light comes on."[3] It is why we must go back there and turn the lights on. The countless Invisible Losses in your life had you go to the memories where you were hurt, to be reminded of the danger in those experiences so you will avoid them in the future. It is possible, for some people, that these Thriver memories were eliminated, as they did not matter in their future of grief and survival of it as much as the memories that would help them avoid future loss and pain.

The easiest way to remember a thriving moment of the past is to look for it in a time that the brain has decided to organize some memories as meaningful. In other words, this memory may be rewritten as a Thriver memory later in life even if it wasn't quite Thriver-like at the time it took place. You decide later that a time spent at the lake house with your family when you were five was a special time, especially if, soon after that period, you experienced a lot of struggles. Therefore, you look back at that time as carefree and fun before a time of hardship unexpectedly took place.

You translate that memory and change its meaning after life taught you lessons. You don't remember it as it was; you remember it as what it meant to you later in life. Finding authentic Thriver memories (without a reward being attached to them in the aftermath of loss) that are purely fun is key to truly remembering your happy existence. So now that you know so much about the way the Survivor-based brain machine has reorganized your life, to be either remembered because of a reward or not remembered because it is not relevant to your survival, you need to go get your Original Self's life back.

Don't ever think that you never had fun. You had fun. You were made to have fun. It was your default setting. The Survivor narrative made up stories to tame you. It called you reckless and shut the door in your face. Let's remember the story the way it was written the first go around. Survivor is a ghostwriter. Never the original voice.

Ready?

Homework Prep: The Bridge to Your Thriver's Past

I have wanted to formally reintroduce you to this part of you for so long, but I had to be patient, as I know that when the Thriver tries to come in too soon, it gets kicked out by Survivor's misguided thoughts. Often Survivor thoughts are activated when the Thriver begins prominently appearing.

Doing your Plug-Ins has helped you become ready to embrace the dreaming, life-loving part of you that is the Thriver. Because you've put some distance between you and your Survivor, you have enough mental space to reconnect to this part of you, which knows laughter, joy, and love.

Traveling back through time and remembering yourself and your emotions during this earlier period will activate the part of you that knows how to thrive, be alive, and feel happy. In this exercise, I am asking you to become familiar with the optimist who always thought of all the good that was possible in life. Let's go find that happy memory from when you were younger. Let's recall it now with this visualization exercise.

Recall Your Thriver Memory

Find a comfortable seat and put your feet up where you can feel the most relaxed. Close your eyes and get cozy. Breathe in deeply and breathe out gently. After you take a couple of these peaceful breaths, drop the weight of your whole body as if you were going to sleep. Drop your shoulders. Let go. Breathe in and out once again, and let's begin the guided portion of your Thriver memory recall.

Imagine that you are looking at a beautiful bridge right in front of you. This bridge could either be a familiar bridge you have walked on or completely imaginary. This bridge will metaphorically carry you back to a time in your past before you ever experienced significant hurt or loss. You will be building a connection between the here and now and the past at a time when you were carefree. As you gently start the walk across the bridge, notice the streetlamps on your left or right that turn on as you walk by them. As you make your way toward this old Thriver memory, the lights will start becoming brighter. You are approaching a time in your life when you just felt good. Take yourself to a memory when you felt and looked happy. Notice what you are wearing. Once you do that, turn your attention all around you. You may be approaching a familiar building and walking inside it. Can you remember something specific on the walls of the space you are in? Is there any art or wallpaper you can remember? Are there people inside that space? Is your mother or father there, maybe wearing a colorful sweater? If you are outside some-where on your own, look for something that stands out. Anything that is grabbing your attention: it could be a memorable building, a bike on the sidewalk, anything at all. Now that you are holding that one thing in your memory, let's spend a few seconds right here; you have arrived at a time when everything felt easy and simple. You may have been a child or a young adult. Remember your smile, your heart's desires, and your love for life. If you are not there yet, go back in time as far as you need to, to find that time.

Remember smiling and how it felt to be alive in that time without loss, fear, or pain. How old were you? What were your thoughts?

Let yourself remember your Original Self during that time. Spend a few minutes living in the past. Is there anything you had forgotten about yourself? What was so fun about you then? Were you an artist, an athlete, or just a fun-loving kid who shared their world with everyone?

The you that you're reconnecting with is your Thriver—the dreamer, adventurer, and lover of life and people. The Thriver's heart is passionate. It wants to give and receive love. Has this memory reminded you of anything that you had completely forgotten about yourself? If the Thriver could talk to you, what would it tell you?

Listen to the thoughts that were present then. Remember what you were doing when you felt the happiest. Stay here for as long as you need to. No rush.

When you are ready, invite this remembered part of you to come back with you across the bridge into the present. As you start the walk back with your new forgotten Thriver memory, you are bringing that part of you back with you. Notice the streetlights brightening up more as you walk by them. As you make your way back across the bridge, seeing the grasslands across the way, are you walking with a different rhythm? Maybe your steps are a little faster, but not necessarily hurried. You're excited to feel this way again after such a long time walking heavily through your daily routine. Imagine that the Thriver is taking you by the hand and wants to start running ahead.

As you arrive in the present moment, feel the ground under your feet, and before you open your eyes, check in and notice how you feel. Is the feeling in your heart different than it was before? Can you see that this part of you was always here, waiting for you to remember it, acknowledge it, and experience it again?

Take a moment to bask in your feelings.

When you're ready, open your eyes.

Record Your Experience
I hope that you are feeling something different, something either forgotten or new. Let's stop here and write down the memory before it can be forgotten again.

- What did you remember?
- What was the biggest surprise once you arrived at the Thriver memory?

- Was there a feeling you felt that you had forgotten about?

- Did the memory choice surprise you? If so, how?

- What did the streetlights do as you went by them?

- What happens every time you visit the Thriver memory?

- What kind of bridge did your mind create for your walk? Was it a bridge you have been to before?

Repeat the Recall

The more often you go over that bridge, spending time recalling Thriver memories, the bigger the library of recalled Thriver memories becomes. Just like the last time, go back to that walk across the bridge to the Thriver memory whenever you feel up to it.

Once there, spend some time revisiting it. Once you feel at home with your Thriver Self, take a new bridge walk to a new Thriver memory. After a while, you will be able to recall the memories one after the other.

....

Homework Prep: Find the Thriver Pattern

Once you access a couple of different Thriver memories, you'll look for their Thriver pattern. They exist in the same way Survivor patterns exist. It is easier for us to access the Survivor patterns because they are such a big and automatic presence in our lives. The Thriver memory pattern is there too; we just have to do extra work to find it. For example, in your Thriver memory, let's say you saw yourself fishing for hours at a time with your dad. Or you saw yourself riding your bike with your friends. Maybe the pattern here is the need for connection while out and about. Or that you thrived when you were spending lots of time outside.

This pattern is crucial in identifying your Original Self, the self that had to be quieted down because you were busy surviving your life. Once you find this pattern, you can use it for your Plug-In design and creating a new Thriver memory, which will become the new foundation of your life. We'll look at how to design the Thriver-focused

Plug-In later in this chapter, but for now let's focus on finding the Thriver pattern.

- Grab a pen and paper and write out at least two Thriver memory recalls from your walks over the bridge.

- Read back and highlight the similarities between them.

- Find the theme, the Thriver pattern. For example, you always look happy when out of the house.

In the next practice, we'll add another step for designing the Plug-In.

In the Thriver Zone

During your Thriver memory recall, you may have noticed something about how intense these experiences were. They felt this way because when you thrive, you are taken away from everything else around you. It is a form of hyperfocus. The Thriver Self can focus intently on adventure and discovery, and in this way, it can impact your brain, even when you connect to the Thriver for a low-risk Plug-In. Up to this point, the only thing that kept your Thriver at bay was being trapped inside the Waiting Room with nothing to play with. It had nothing to occupy its mind, as everything in the Waiting Room was low risk for the kid-like self who wanted to play all day long. Remember when you were a child who could go on and on playing outside in the yard, seemingly forever? When you had no concept of time passing, you were so engaged with what you were doing? We want to get just a little of this back so we can integrate it with the whole self.

Keep in mind that the Thriver's hyperfocus superpower is not to be used full-time, as it will derail all the other less interesting activities in your life that are still important, such as driving your kids to school, paying your bills, and finishing that work project. Life outside of the Waiting Room still has these parts of life, and unfortunately, we can't completely ignore them.

So we'll have to harness that Thriver power. But before we do that, we will rev it up as much as humanly possible—it has, after all, been sleeping for quite some time. Let's regain our ability to thrive for a longer stretch of time. The Thriver's hyperfocus superpower is still at play even if you start with a low-risk Plug-In, as long as it is something that can be fun for that Thriver kid inside you.

Another way to look at this is that the Survivor Self has the same hyperfocus ability—it is just that the focus is on the fear and not on the fun. The difference is that the Thriver hyperfocus is a natural state, and when you are born with it, you don't need to activate it or trigger it in any way. It just is. Once your inner narrative is reframed, you focus on fun and play, certainly not fear. *You just express yourself. You just create. You are just being in the moment.* Remember, the Thriver hyperfocus is in the present. The Survivor is always derived from a loss in the past, even though it is speaking to you in the present moment. You see, the Survivor has the Waiting Room as a home, where it can supercharge its powers. That is why we have to make a home for your Thriver too, so it can keep getting stronger. Otherwise, this is an unfair fight.

Rene's Thriver Discovery

Rene was a fifty-year-old CPA who had been the main provider for her family. Her husband was diagnosed with a form of blindness that had placed him on long-term disability when the kids were young. Rene had to become the breadwinner and the one responsible for her family's budget, as well as the decision-maker when it came to family vacations. She had taken my Life Reentry class once before and got a lot out of it, but she still found herself going back to the Waiting Room of her Invisible Loss of safety.

When her husband lost part of his sight, she found herself worrying about her family becoming homeless. Of course, this was a reaction to her husband's inability to make a living, but it was also a survival reaction to her Invisible Loss of her father having to work three jobs when she was young, so she never really saw him or spent any time with him.

Whenever she would go to her dad, he was always busy with something, and he would tell her that she should be grateful that he had these jobs so she would not have to be homeless.

Every time Rene missed him, she invalidated that feeling within herself by saying that he was working to put a roof over her head. Now, as an adult, not only was Rene worried about not providing enough for her family, but she also worried that her kids would miss her the way she had missed her dad. So she never spent any time looking after herself, as she would make sure she spent all her free time with her kids.

Rene's husband became a stay-at-home dad, as he was still able to take care of the kids inside the home with his limited eyesight. Even though Rene made sure she provided for her family like her dad had, while making sure that her kids did not feel abandoned, she ended up abandoning herself. She still never gave herself the love and attention she needed as a child.

Not only did she not give it to herself, but she never let anyone else give it to her either. Her role in the family, with both her husband and children, was that of a caretaker. She was never the one taken care of.

Rene's true Invisible Loss was self-care. She was the most vulnerable there. She did not want to experience rejection from anyone and, consequently, never asked for what she needed. She also never wanted to acknowledge that her need for attention was as important as her need to provide it for others. While we were in a week of the class that focused on discovery of the Thriver, Rene surprised us all by booking a trip for herself to Venice, Italy.

She had apparently booked this trip three times before but always canceled it. The Survivor Self had managed to convince her that this was too expensive and too self-indulgent. The thing is that the Plug-Ins prior to the booking of the trip were not getting her closer to the shift from the Survivor to the Watcher. So she had experienced the shift toward the Original Self. She also had never really accessed her own wisdom in the Watcher activation exercise. Her Reframes stayed mechanical, and her Cleanses never moved to the Watcher voice. She could not truly write directly from her Watcher Self.

But this time she designed small self-care Plug-Ins that would make her feel calm. She went for a massage after ten years of not having one. She stayed in bed for a whole morning over the weekend. By this time, the kids were out of the house and in college. But she also chose these Plug-Ins by what she craved. Which was different from what she had done before, choosing them based on what she thought she needed.

So when the trip came about, she chose to go, as her Daily Stacks were pointing her toward a shift that told her that she could budget for self-care the same way she budgeted for food. Her husband decided to stay home; he was never into travel in the first place. Rene had to be honest with herself that she had used her husband as an excuse for not traveling, even though he had never asked her to stay back and had assured her he could manage on his own. We all know that this was her Survivor making sure she didn't take the risk of going on these trips.

Once there, she discovered that she liked the language enough to want to learn as much as she could during her trip. When she got back, she decided to continue learning and plan another trip for the next year. She was a planner, after all. Her hyperfocus on learning a language allowed her to make plans for more travel in her life. All of a sudden, she started dressing differently, identifying with a different wardrobe palette from dark colors to muted hues of pink and green.

She discovered that her Original Self had always wanted to connect and communicate, but when her dad was not able to do that with her, she surrounded herself with numbers, budgets, and responsibilities that kept her head down. Her Original Self was curious and had many questions for her dad, questions that always remained unanswered.

Rene finally reentered her life with a new language and new travel adventures. She ultimately started to work with companies based in the United States but with international offices that needed financial services. She incorporated Italy into her business and no longer dreaded coming back from her travels to her Waiting Room life. She moved her whole life out of the Waiting Room after the discoveries she made along the way. She said, "I can't talk myself out of this anymore. I now want to feel like this in every part of my life."

How to Design the Thriver-Focused Plug-In
You are finally considering the present as the most important part of your life. Now you understand why the Thriver Self can only live here. It is not like the Watcher and Survivor. They can go back and forth in time. The Thriver is only alive in the present. The longer you stay here,

the stronger it will get. All you have to do is plug in to the hyperfocused Thriver and ride the wave of thriving for as long as you can.

That is when you let go without having to let go. This feels good. Finally. It is better than where you used to be in silence, isolated in the Waiting Room. You are now closer to understanding why you had to abandon your Thriver zone for so long. You are finding yourself in a place where, after acknowledging your Invisible Losses and plugging in to the life they were hiding from you, you are ready to feel safe to thrive once again. At first, for just a few moments. Let's see how this can take place.

You are about to take a bigger step toward your final exit from the Waiting Room. At last, you can open the door wide with the super-charged and hyperfocused Thriver Plug-In. This is possible because your Stack has been able to advocate for good communication skills between your Watcher Self and Thriver Self as you were deciding on all your prior Plug-Ins. You can now finally depend on the Thriver to carry you through—not only stepping out of the Waiting Room for short esca-pades but also for the longer trip out.

Let's break it down a bit further.

You start to cleanse as you'd normally do for your Daily Stacks. But today you start your Stack with the Thriver voice. When you listen in, you find yourself excited about a Plug-In you are thinking about. You stay there. You write about that for as long as you need to. If your Survivor tries to butt in, you spot it quickly with your Watcher and kick it out without even having to do the whole reframe. You are now in the mastery of your discovery step. This is the result of daily Cleanses and Stacks for a few weeks in a row. The Plug-Ins have been shifting your thoughts and moving you from a fixation on worry to a focus on play. It is a strong Stack to be in.

Your Stack becomes supercharged. This time you don't think of the risk the same way you used to. You think of the playfulness of it. You choose the time and the place, and you now go and make it happen. But before you do, you must do a final check to see if this is the right Plug-In for the Thriver hyperfocus to come into play.

Design the Plug-In

For example, if you remembered a beautiful hike with an old friend where you camped out, ask yourself which part of that memory was the most joyful and fun. If it was the actual hiking, how did it feel to hike for a few hours; how did your body respond? If it was the camping with the friend and the connection you made during that time, then is there a Plug-In that can transport you to a similar feeling? It does not have to be hiking or camping but something that resembles this form of adventure. You can now do a Conversation Stack just on this. As your Survivor will try to sabotage this Thriver memory creation, you will need to enable the Conversation Stack (the conversation among the three selves). Here's an example:

SURVIVOR: Don't you remember how you fell and injured your ankle during that trip? Why would you want to do that again?

WATCHER: I remember that fall, but I also remember how much fun it was to camp out that night in front of the fire. I felt like we were being courted by the stars all night long. As a matter of fact, this memory has been one of my favorites, and I am so glad I am recalling it now.

THRIVER: Let's plan something fun, even if it is sitting out on the deck with a candle, listening to my favorite music and chatting with an old friend (low-risk Plug-In). It's been way too long. When I spend time outdoors, I feel like I can do anything.

What Survivor Behavior Is It Replacing?

Let's go back to look at Rene's story.

Her Thriver Plug-In was born out of the low-risk Plug-In, and once she got enough courage to risk more, she got on that plane to Venice. The opposite of that Plug-In was the Waiting Room behavior that had her not having any free time for travel.

The Thriver is always hidden behind the Survivor. The things we resist the most are normally the things the Survivor is afraid will tempt us out of the Waiting Room. Rene knew that if she traveled, she would have such a hard time coming back to her life that she never allowed herself to do it. So this is how we look for the opposite behavior in the Waiting Room, and when we find it, we know we are headed in the right direction. Yes, this is a high-risk Plug-In, but you are finally in a place of wanting to risk your current life for more moments of play.

Coffee Break

I know you have been doing a lot of reentering in the last few pages. Have you noticed that lately you have been putting your feet up more often? And not just for the Thriver recall exercises. You seem more relaxed. Your hair may be a little messier, in a good way.

You haven't felt like this in quite some time. The air has been changing. You seem lighter. I sense a different presence. You seem to have more time. And remember, happiness is personal. It is a journey as unique as the way you look. What an honor it has been to walk with you on the journey of Life Reentry. I remember clearly your first pages with me, when the Survivor was the loudest voice and the creator of your life. Also the key holder of the Waiting Room. Now the keys belong to the Thriver and the Watcher Self. During this time together, I have seen you exit the Waiting Room many times. I have seen you laugh and cry all at once. I have seen you experience a journey of transformation throughout these pages. We have shared so much together, and you have worked so hard to get here.

Reentry is not just a process; it is a way of life. Once you have completed a round, it is time to go into maintenance mode. You might even experience the whole Life Reentry process in one day if you are dealing with an Invisible Loss taking place in a friendship during a tough conversation.

Or when you get rejected at work and not considered for a promotion, for example. In other words, activate a routine process of reentry following an Invisible Loss, as the Survivor Self will surely take over the narrative during these times. But the difference now is that when you visit the Waiting Room, it's more a place of refuge than hiding. You now have control over how long you stay.

We all have very quirky ways of experiencing happiness. The more Invisible Loss you have experienced, the more tailored your happiness will need to be. We can have the same kind of rejections, the same humiliation stories, the same heartbreaks. We may visit the same places. Walk the same roads. Look at the same views. But our feelings of happiness will not be found at the same exact moment as everyone else's. Don't look for them there. Go after your own version of what feels good. Even if it is a half-painted wall in your kitchen. Or a strange-looking chair with five legs. Maybe even a dish of plain spaghetti. OK, here is where you will define what your Life Reentry looks like. As you know by now, Life Reentry after Invisible Loss is not the same as other losses. This is an intricate, complex process of redefining what happiness is for you now. What truly makes you come alive. Always remember that this definition is not static; it changes with each Life Reentry journey.

Life Reentry is the feeling of taking a big breath and letting it fill your lungs with oxygen. Life Reentry is a slow walk next to the ocean. It is being happy to wake up in the morning. Or the ability to allow for rest in the midst of a hard day. Life Reentry is often choosing to not worry about the future. It may simply be a good friend coming over for dinner.

Life Reentry is a swim in the middle of the night. Life Reentry is sitting with your dog when your partner just left you. It is the simplest of things, never the mightiest of dreams or the biggest of leaps. And without rest in between, you can't make these reentries into your life happen. It's essential to rest in between all of your thriving days. So let's see what a *planned* Waiting Room day looks like.

A Planned Waiting Room Day

If you don't go back to the Waiting Room when your new neural pathways are still weak, no matter how rebellious and ready to change your life you are, you will be taken out by the Survivor. If, for example, you keep plugging in without giving yourself a safe break, and you don't give yourself the opportunity to cleanse what is happening, to see how the Survivor brain is trying to hold you back, you won't last long.

Imagine being in the army. You are on the battlefield, and you are losing the battle. Your Watcher Self, your commander, is asking everyone to pull back so they can regroup, as they are all going to be taken out otherwise. This is the same thing. You have to regroup, and doing it in the Waiting Room, utilizing it to fight the biggest enemy of your life, is very smart.

In a sense, you go to the old pathways that you know inside out, you walk on them, and you witness their build. You reframe them with a new thought narrative, one that can fight the enemy and win the battle.

Then, you go back out.

What does a Waiting Room day look like? It could look as simple as taking a day off: You watch a good TV show. You don't shower until later. You don't plug in to anything that feels difficult. You don't create. You don't brush your hair if you don't want to. You don't care for yourself in any way that requires work. You just do what you need to do to rest in the way that feels good to you. Or maybe rest looks like self-care for you, so maybe instead you go for a pedicure, or you get dressed up. Whatever works for you. You don't go out in the sun if bright light is too much for you. You hibernate. Away from life. Away from tough conversations. Explorations. New spaces. Experiences. The only part you need to maintain is your thoughts.

Remember, your Original Self has the answer to this, and it's a combination of Watcher and Thriver. If you feel like your Survivor is asleep, do a Conversation Stack just with your Watcher and Thriver and listen in for that integrated Original Self voice. For example:

WATCHER: Do you remember the time when the schedule wasn't set? And you would just wake up and figure things out along the way? Wouldn't that be a fun day to have?

THRIVER: Oh, I remember, and if you ask me, I would have a couple of these days; just one is not enough. Why don't I move some things around and make it happen? Maybe I can do my Waiting Room day this weekend and move that work function out of the way and clear up both days; it normally takes me a while to get going with doing nothing.

ORIGINAL INTEGRATED SELF: I work better when I take the weekends off completely, making them unscheduled. As a matter of fact, I will clear up the following weekend as well and see if we can make that the norm going forward.

At this juncture, it is important to start to glimpse the integration happening at the end of these Conversation Stacks. The truth of your Original Self rests right here.

While in Waiting Room mode, you must maintain the basic Life Reentry stack. You must stay out of Survivor thinking even if everything else is in Waiting Room mode. Cleanse, pattern spot, reframe. No difficult Plug-Ins when you are in rest mode in the Waiting Room. Be aware, while in there, that you have chosen to go there willingly. You are not captive to it; you are not fooled by it. You can walk out whenever you want. You are in charge.

In some cases, you won't have the luxury of time to go back and regroup, but when you do, you must listen to the Watcher, who knows your strengths and your weaknesses, and do what you have to do for the long-term fight. This is not one and done. This is not just a quick fix; this is a way of life. When you find yourself in the Waiting Room for a longer period, and you are struggling, you will need to put in extra time with the Life Reentry practice. You will need to look for what is invisible in your life, what is breaking your heart that you can't quite see. Remember, there is a reason why we call them Invisible Losses; they hide deep inside of us. Then you will do the Cleanse, and you will take your time with it. Let it all spill out; write it out. Don't let anything be buried. Or hidden. Even from you.

Your Reframe may feel a little difficult at first if you are experiencing a new loss, but stay with it, and try to listen to what the Watcher is trying to remind you of. When the time comes, only plug in at a low risk. Don't challenge yourself if you have been in the Waiting Room for a few days.

Do you remember how slowly we started? You must always go slow.

Homework: Thriver Day

When you go about your day today, remember that you will have to write about it through your Thriver Self. As you move through your schedule at work or at home, pay attention to moments that bring a smile to your face or when you feel unexpected joy. Just note it down on your phone if you don't have anything else nearby. At the end of your day, look over your Thriver notes and write about your day through your Thriver voice. This is not about your planned Plug-Ins and how they made you feel but about a natural way to thrive without the Stack at play. Without the Reframes or any of the tools we used. This is about your Thriver's current default setting. Have you managed to get yourself to a place where you naturally thrive?

Chapter 8

Final Integration

A t this point, the Survivor Self is no longer overseeing your wishes, your dreams, nor the direction of your life. Now the wanting and wishing are being experienced by the Watcher and Thriver, with a sprinkle of the Survivor since, as you know by now, we can't ever be rid of this Survivor Self completely. But it is finally lessened and blended in as you have started to trust the voice of your Original Self more and more. As you are now integrating the three selves, you are beginning to have faith in your future once again and starting to trust the timing of your life. You may not have all the answers, but the longer you walk on this path and continue to trust yourself, the more the answers will find their way to you.

You now have a better understanding of what makes you (Original Self) happy and what doesn't. You realized that ignoring the truth of that was not healthy or good for you, and you now know that the difficulty of starting a new life may not be as hard as trying to hold on to the old one. Whoever you've been, whoever you are becoming, be ready for who you could be next. Be gentle with yourself, especially as this final phase of integration can be hard, because when you change a few things in your life, everything around those things will also rise to meet that change. You have courageously done the work, and now you are ready to claim that shift once and for all and make it a sustainable part of you.

We are now bringing your Watcher Reframes, Cleanses, and Thriver Plug-Ins together in a clear and concrete way so you have an awareness and a certainty not only about the changes you have made so far but also about who you really are due to these shifts and revelations. You may be less afraid to speak your mind; you are appreciative of your surroundings; your thoughts are a little quieter and at peace, even if the noise around you is still present. Most important, you enjoy your own company. You may be craving learning new skills just for fun and not for success or glory. Maybe you understand others better because you know that everyone has their own Survivor to deal with. And even if you don't feel like you are quite there yet, I am here to remind you that you are certainly on your way. So let's step further into the shifts you made and the newfound identity of the Original Self that is showing its face more and more. Let's now revisit the Original Self–Inventory Scale to note and take stock of the shifts and changes you made. It is time to put all the remaining pieces of the puzzle together and measure your incredible growth.

....

Homework: The Original Self-Inventory Scale

As you maneuvered your way out of the Waiting Room, by stacking the Cleanses, Patterns, Reframes, and Plug-Ins, you were carefully putting your Original Self back together again. Integrating who you came into this life to be with the wisdom you have garnered from your Watcher and the playfulness of your Thriver. When you look back on your Plug-Ins and the Reframes that led you to them, you get to witness your newfound boundaries, self-trust, and knowledge about who you truly are and how you have already started to show up in your own life outside the Waiting Room.

You already know so much about your rediscovered Original Self, emerging from the divergent self as it got to explore the Thriver and solidifying its presence by acknowledging and validating the shifts that have occurred. These shifts jolted you further out of the Waiting Room. If we don't validate them and make them part of the whole, it will be much easier for the Survivor Self to convince you otherwise.

Let's gather all the evidence we can and capture all that has been discovered so far. We have moved from witnessing, processing, understanding, and experimenting to shifting and discovering and finally to reentering. Let's begin the integration part by asking your Original Self the same inventory questions you were asked in the beginning for more clarity on changes that you've been making for yourself as you've progressed through your Life Reentry practice. Make sure you are generous with yourself as you add your numbers for each question.

- Self-Trust: After multiple Moments of Impact, time in the Waiting Room, and consistent Survivor-based behavior, you have finally begun to trust yourself again. What do you now trust about yourself that you did not previously? How has your self-confidence grown? Before adding your new self-trust number, consider what it was at the beginning of the journey. Then, add your new number between 0 (not trusting) and 10 (very trusting).

  My Self-Trust Number is ___.

- Healthy Boundaries: As you have further connected to your relationships and stopped people-pleasing or dysfunctional Survivor patterns at work, what new relationship or work boundaries have you established? Compared to your initial boundaries number, how far along the scale has it moved? From 0 (extremely hazardous limits) to 10 (extremely healthful limits).

  My Healthy Boundaries Number is ___.

- Self-Acceptance: You are now beginning to comprehend and accept your past decisions and choices. What aspects of your past and time spent in the Waiting Room have you accepted? How has it evolved on a scale from 0 (no self-acceptance) to 10 (very self-accepting)?

  My Self-Acceptance Number is ___.

- Radical Self-Honesty: Consider how your access to your own knowledge and the truth has improved. Why is it crucial to maintain access to the Watcher in order to notice Survivor thoughts that continue to surface in our daily inner dialogue? That is, what is one Survivor thought you still carry with you? And what does your Watcher think about it? Just like that, you do a quick Stack to get back to that truth. What is your progress when it comes to honesty with yourself? From 0 (not honest) to 10 (very honest).

  My Radical Self-Honesty Number is ___.

- The Present Moment: How does the present feel for you right now? How does it feel to pause, take a deep breath, and experience what it's like to be you in the here and now after this voyage we've been on? Is it easier to be in your life in this moment in time? From 0 (it feels really hard) to 10 (not hard at all), what is your new number?

  My Present Moment Number is ___.

- Giant Leap: What was the most significant change that brought you closer to your Original Self? Which experience generated by a Plug-In took you significantly further from the Waiting Room? What has changed in your capacity to take risks and move forward? From 0 (not improved) to 10 (very improved).

  My Giant Leap Number is ___.

- Compassion Toward Others: Has your increased self-compassion led to an increase in your compassion for others? How has this affected your relationship with them, if so? From 0 (not improved) to 10 (very improved).

  My Compassion Toward Others Number is ___.

- Compassion Toward Self: If you no longer blame yourself for when others abandoned you, that is worth a couple of points at the very least. And if you can now understand the reasoning behind some of your Survivor behaviors that could have hurt others, you are way up that scale, closer to 9 or 10. Self-forgiveness is much easier when there is self-compassion. From 0 (not improved) to 10 (very improved).

My Compassion Toward Self Number is ___.

Here are some additional thoughts that can guide you to the right place on the scale.

- If you have forgiven yourself for all the choices your Survivor labeled as "wrongs," you are moving up the scale at least 2 or 3 points.

- If you don't feel as if your scale has really moved up in number much for yourself, do a good Cleanse, Pattern, Reframe, and Stack on this. Sometimes our Survivor Self holds on to every part of us, but the practice you have created can absolutely overtake that last attempt of the Survivor to have the last word. You got this.

Add up all the numbers and write the total score right here: *My new Original Self-Inventory Score is ___.*

Now you can absolutely compare it to the score you gave yourself at the beginning of the book and see the changes you have made in your life more accurately.

....

Coffee Break

After adding up the scores and becoming more understanding about your past and what you need to do going forward, you may have some lingering grief. There is a devastating but timely lateness to the awareness of your wisdom, and so you may still need to sit with all the questions that are coming in from this last part of the homework. Write about what you are feeling right now in your Cleanses. Give these feelings to the Watcher. Look for what is emerging. You have been in survival mode for so long that you had to keep in your life what was good enough, grateful for some ease. But you no longer have the same needs as before.

The previously unattended portions of your life are asking for their own reentry.

I know what you are thinking. *Oh no, not this too.*

But yes, *this too*. Especially this.

Haven't I worked enough already?

When you hear those words, go and empty your drawers, your closets. Go through the lingering junk—both literally and metaphorically. Everything must go. Be done with all the parts of your life that won't let you stand up straight.

You need to lighten the load. The good news is, this Life Reentry road map you have in your hands will let you know what's coming ahead.

Of course, you will have to fill in the blanks.

This is a personal journey, after all, but it will keep you from getting lost.

Now that you see your life from a new perspective, is there something that no longer belongs? For example, is there a relationship that is good enough but doesn't make you as happy as it used to? Ask yourself, why is that relationship not something you are willing to let go of yet?

For instance, this could be about your doctor, whom you have been seeing for some years. Now she no longer listens to your complaints and always rushes out the door. You feel that you need to stay with your doctor (Survivor feeling), *as she knows you best and you are feeling too embarrassed to cancel your next annual checkup.* Instead, you are going to handle that discomfort; you have trained yourself to do so. You will begin to plug in with looking for a new doctor by asking a couple of your neighbors and friends if they have a referral. You will start with the easy stuff, don't forget, and if you don't know what that first Plug-In should be, go back to do another Stack tomorrow. You will get there. I am certain of it. By the way, this was our last coffee break; now we are on our way to the finish line.

Look at us still here doing the work.

This next part is my favorite, and I hope it will be yours too.

Homework: Your Mission Statement

This next assignment is for you to write your life's mission statement. A list of nonnegotiables about your life. A reminder of all the work you have done over the course of this book. Your life's mission statement will be made from your goals, beliefs, and wisdom. It is a declaration of your Thriver's intentions. It will declare who you are to the world. It will spell out your new identity.

It will remind you of all the new ways you have reclaimed your life. And above all, it will inspire you every day to thrive.

Let's begin.

Write as many words as you need to about your declaration of Life Reentry. Your nonnegotiables. You can create a list of numbered sentences that are bold and connected to the values of your present life. There should be urgency in your words. Thriver-like statements. Profound and sincere. Your mission statement needs to be a sure way out of the Waiting Room when you feel like you need some inspiration. If you struggle to find the words, look back at your Reframes and your Plug-Ins, and you will be able to complete your mission statement with plenty of nonnegotiables.

Here is an example of Rene's mission statement:

I am worthy of happiness.

I no longer doubt my need for connection. When I hear that Survivor voice telling me I don't need to care for myself, I will reframe it with "I prioritize myself because I am worth it."

I travel the world until my legs can't take me anymore. I open myself up to new experiences with my family beyond the daily routine I share with them.

I remember to take deep breaths. I remember to connect with my husband about his day, every day.

I will savor the unconditional love my husband has for me and never take it for granted.

I will no longer waste time worrying about money.

Life is not all work. Life is a game to play.

I spend time learning new skills for no reason.

I am free.

Once your mission statement is written, save it somewhere that is easily accessible. Print it and put it on your fridge if you need to see it in your physical reality versus the digital one. Put it inside a bold frame. Do whatever feels right to celebrate your declarations and to have this inspiring reminder of Thriver's intentions, which will also get you closer to that Original Self of yours.

....

A Definite Change in the Air

The mission statement is the first glimpse of your Original Self attempting to integrate itself into your existence. It originated from all the Mental Stacks, in particular from the Reframe section. You are about to embark on a new chapter of your life, and to bring this Life Reentry practice to a powerful conclusion, I want to emphasize the palpable shift in energy that permeates the room. A new frequency that supersedes the one you were in. Change of this size can feel overwhelming, but it wouldn't be coming for you if it did not belong to you. It is part of a new world that was built for you, by you, and you will be there to meet it. Just remember, you are here to live more than one life, to love more than the people you already do, and to do it all, at the same time, certainly not *after* or *later*, not someday, but now. You are ready to embark on your journey in the midst of your hard day or in the middle of your OK job. You can plug in after a breakup, an argument with your mom, your sister's meltdown, or while your bank account is empty.

Especially then. Go on.

If you don't know which way to go next, read your life's mission statement, do a Mental Stack, and go plug in to the direction your Original Self is sending you. Remember, it's been waiting to take this journey for a really long time, so don't pause for too long; the Survivor Self is never far away.

You got this. I see you, just as you were always meant to be seen.

Conclusion

You Have the Last Words

Finally, after a long journey, seeing yourself through the hardest parts of your life, you have spent this time bringing into being the person you were always meant to be. Dare I say, it was almost impossible to track and reclaim the unscathed Original Self. But you've done it. Let's pause briefly now and assess your journey.

You have now tasted the freedom that comes from getting to know yourself outside the daily grind of the Waiting Room. You may have even arrived at a place where you don't care what anyone says or thinks of you. It is the most freeing human experience to discover this place, isn't it? This place of reentry where you can trust your own choices enough to keep moving in the direction of your Original Self. Almost like an homage to your soul's journey.

This work has always been about you remembering who you are and protecting that Original Self when your heart breaks. It is a different kind of protection than the one the Survivor Self is occupied with. This is about nurturing the smile on your face. The tenderness in your heart. The excitement of the simple everyday things.

The coffeepot in the morning. The present sense of your existence where nothing is missing from the past, and you don't think about what the future could add. That moment where you sit still, captivated by what is taking place in your living room.

And if you have young children, and you hear them playing, even though your long list of to-dos is calling you, you still manage to make a memory of that precious moment. A memory of a moment in time, a moment where your home sounds like a giggle. That memory of your children feeling joy gets to stay with you whenever your Survivor Self tries to delete anything that doesn't serve the need to keep you in the Waiting Room.

You also cleanse the Survivor voice when you have a hard day at work.

Your Watcher steps in and tells you more about that hard day with reminders of your Thriver's past and how you had fun on a rainy day before. Your Survivor, of course, tries to meddle by telling you that it is not that simple. But you are now not as gullible, and you push back with your words, responding, *Well, of course, it is that simple. A hard day doesn't make for a hard life.*

For the days when you are afraid to plug in to your truth, you now trust that it is part of the process, and you go back to your Cleanses, finding the pattern of fear that is still acting up. And you turn the volume down by taking the lowest-risk step you can take so you can keep walking out of that prison. Staying stuck in that fear response makes everything else scarier than it is.

There are no scary monsters on the other side of the Plug-In. You find yourself laughing at that last sentence, shaking your head for believing the exaggerations of your primitive brain keeping you safe and scared within the illusion of wholeness. Now, of course, you can tell the difference between your Original Self and the Survivor version of you. What was invisible before is now revealed. You know who stole your sense of self. The truth of your gifts. The specialness of your unique voice. The destined trajectory is reestablished. You are now finally back on track. Making your discoveries along the way, at last. Finding the treasures that have been waiting for you all these years.

Grief of this kind does what it is here to do. It heals the lost time. It makes the present longer. It puts you in charge of the clocks. It slows everything down enough for you to take what has always been yours and thrive. Remember that first story you told me about your life? I bet you can now sit and rewrite it.

How you found your way back to your Original Self's life, courageously making up for lost time because now you know how to come back from heartbreak whenever you need to. It is always going to be the journey between the invisible and the seen. The imprisoning of self and the freedom of it. The practice of Life Reentry keeps you free for longer stretches. You stack your Survivor thoughts against your Watcher and Thriver ones. Reframing them to fit the true story of your life. Here's to that.

Acknowledgments

I could not have undertaken this journey without my family. To my daughters, Elina and Isabel, for being wiser than their young years, my life is forever yours. To my husband, Eric, who has been by my side from the beginning of this journey, helping me trust myself when I doubted my skills and abilities as a writer and teacher.

To my parents, Nikos and Despina, and my sister, Artemis, who are always proud of my choices and dedication to this work. To my treasured friends, who supported me during the long and hard years of writing this book: Nathalie and Joel Dolisy, Shannon Quinn, Dr. Melissa Rowe, Gilden Tunador, Dr. Lyn Boyd-Judson, Frank White, Elaine Glass, Michael Fishman, Julie Jarvie, Jayne Dakin, Dr. Raymond Sanchez, Kristine Carlson, Erin Matlock, Michelle Steinke-Baumgard, Zeta Papastrati, and Jenny Thompson. To the Solar sisters, thank you Loretta Whiteshades, Dr. Camille Alleyne, Mary Liz Bender, Dr. Sian Proctor, Hillary Coe, Yasmine El Baggari, and Kelly Larson for all the mid-book adventures.

To my therapist, Andrea Redman, for her weekly insights and support as I was on this journey. I thank the members of my team, Courtney and Justin, who have been with me for the past few years, in plenty of highs and lows.

I would like to express my deepest gratitude to my editors, Angela Wix, Diana Ventimiglia, and Jennifer Kasius, for their relentless help with the manuscript. Each one of you played an important part in this book, and it was extraordinary to see the results as all the pieces came together. To my literary agent, Jan Baumer, who supported the book in its early stages, especially during the challenging times. To the Sounds True team for their commitment to excellence.

To all the participants who attended the Life Reentry classes from 2011 to 2022: without their passion and drive to reenter their own lives, I would not have been able to find my way to the discovery of Invisible Loss. You all have played a part in validating the content of this book through your homework assignments and your honest responses to your personal experiences.

Lastly, I am grateful to the many guides, seen and unseen, who have always held my hand from the beginning of my writing journey until this moment.

Appendix: Support Group Guide

It is not the suffering that creates Invisible Loss
but the lack of a witness to the suffering.

This appendix provides information that can be used as an Invisible Loss and Life Reentry support group guide by anyone who wishes to form a group. You can also use this guide as a solitary reader to tackle the book in a weekly format, but without a group environment.

Who This Guide Is For

Use this guide if you are a professional who is running any type of emotional support group in your private practice, in a medical setting, or for example, within a community for veteran services, caregiver services, cancer support services, traditional group support for grief from divorce or death, domestic abuse centers, or prisons.

If you are not a licensed professional, then it is important to have been a part of a Life Reentry support group prior to facilitating.

Purpose and Target Audience

Your support group is for people who have experienced a specific Invisible Loss, such as loss of identity, purpose, or carefree living, or are experiencing increased anxiety and dread following, for example, a cardiovascular disease, cancer, autoimmune disease, or other medical life-changing diagnosis. It could also be about new parents, new retirees, or new college graduates. Anyone who may be feeling trapped in their life, relationship, or job and anyone who is unsure of the cause of their struggle. So long as the group shares experiences or faces similar obstacles.

About a Life Reentry Support Group

A Life Reentry support group assists individuals in different types of Invisible Loss to rebuild their lives. The weekly meetings are structured around the five phases of Life Reentry. Each group member initially must read *Invisible Loss* on their own or go through the book while in the group setting.

In traditional loss, the Life Reentry process takes off where Kübler-Ross[1] (the author of the five stages of grief) leaves us, when the grieving, denial, and all the anger and emotions have been experienced for a while. The material in *Invisible Loss* meets the group participants sometimes years after their Moment of Impact and Primary Invisible Loss while still in anger, denial, and angst but without knowing the why behind these emotions. Each week guides the participant from the initial tracking and discovery of Primary Invisible Losses to the reclaiming of the Original Self and the experience of moments of Life Reentry.

The Life Reentry Support Group Focus

Traditionally, participants in support groups often remain in the Waiting Room for years, reliving and retelling Survivor-based stories. Unfortunately, there is insufficient life-oriented follow-up to enable individuals to rebuild their lives outside of the Waiting Room. Unintentionally, some support groups allow past loss to dominate the conversation that should ideally be about life and how to start fully living and thriving after any kind of loss. I have found that there are no other support groups for those Moments of Impact that lead to Invisible Loss; this type of group serves the purpose of filling that gap that derives from societal misconceptions. Over the years, some Life Reentry group participants have shared that they felt guilty when they were ready to leave the typical grief support groups they belonged to, feeling ashamed to be creating new life stories. Life Reentry support groups can remove the stigma from suffering and help group members validate loss in any type of transition.

Structure of Life Reentry Group Meetings

There are two types of Life Reentry support groups. The first is the introductory nine-week structure, in which participants undergo the Life Reentry process outlined in *Invisible Loss*. The second type is the Life Reentry Maintenance support group, which takes off at the end of a first round of Life Reentry, starting at Week 10.

If you have read *Invisible Loss* and completed the assignments on your own, or if you have participated in a nine-week Life Reentry support group, you may enroll in a Maintenance group. The duration of both Introductory Life Reentry and Maintenance support groups should be ninety minutes per week or every other week. If you do not know anyone locally or online who is operating a group or using the tools in this book, please visit lifereentry.com or invisiblelosses.com to let us know that you are searching for a group or that you would like to add your own group to our list of resources.

Nine-Week Group Support Structure

This nine-week group schedule is to run alongside the book *Invisible Loss*, as each week corresponds to specific chapters. When beginning Life Reentry, most participants are not in a perspective of growth. Rather, in most cases, they are absorbed by the Survivor Self narrative and will need the specific Life Reentry exercises and prompts to begin. The group is set up in a way that allows participant members to reposition themselves in order to strengthen new patterns of thought and behavior. Each week has a clear intention and perspective that create a safe container for each participant. Each week begins with instruction for each Life Reentry phase and its specific concept followed by participant interaction, either online or in person. Online interaction in between meetings is very beneficial if it can be maintained through online support groups, for example, Facebook groups or other virtual settings. Part of the healing and validating element of the Life Reentry support group derives from the acknowledgment received from other participants. These interactions reinforce the reemergence of the Original Self. Each session ends with a clear intention for the week and specific action-oriented homework that participants commit to completing and sharing with one another online or in person.

Week 1: Introductions
This week focuses on introductions and participants sharing their story as it stands right now, familiarizing themselves with one another.

Reading: Introduction

Objectives:

- Articulate clear expectations for weekly in-person sessions or virtual meetings.

- Encourage validation of each participant's Baseline Story telling. Foster a nonjudgmental environment in which all participants feel comfortable sharing vulnerable Moments of Impact.

- Discussion of Original Self, Waiting Room, and Invisible Loss central ideas.

Group Share: Baseline Story Exercise. Request that participants introduce themselves and share their Baseline Story with the group. What was their reason for joining the group?

Group Support: Ask group members to show support by responding to each other's shared stories online or in person while in the group.

Homework:

- Share Baseline Story in writing in online group and comment on the stories of others with compassion and validation.

- Complete Original Self-Inventory Scale.

Week 2: Awareness Phase—Origin of the Survivor Self from Invisible Loss
During this week, group participants will be looking back at their lives and reviewing possible Moments of Impact. Week 2 is structured around

the Invisible Loss discovery exercises and a basic introduction of Survivor, Watcher, and Thriver Selves. Reading:

Chapter 1: The Waiting Room

Objectives:

- How do we get stuck in the Waiting Room, and what is the Waiting Room mindset?
- What is the origin of the Survivor Self?
- Get to know the Survivor Self and how it makes itself known.

Group Share: Group participants share possible Invisible Losses with one another, following the guidelines from chapter 1.

Group Support: Participants in the group share their first impressions of what Invisible Loss is and how it pertains to their lives. With verbal validation and acknowledgment, the group creates the space to greet, process, and validate one another during the sharing of an Invisible Loss for the very first time.

Homework: Trace the Invisible Loss from adulthood in between Weeks 2 and 3 and share in online forum with the rest of the group.

Week 3: Awareness Phase—The Fragmented Self
During Week 3, group participants are getting to know how their Original Self could have been separated from them. They are gaining glimpses through the filters of their three distinct selves so that the early Invisible Loss memory can be discovered. This week, we pay attention to the concept of the Watcher. A self-aware inner voice that guides these mindset shifts. Participants are given a guided visualization exercise to help develop the Watcher Self.

Reading: Chapter 2: The Fragmented Self—Survivor, Watcher, Thriver

Objectives:

- Get to know the Watcher Self and how it makes itself known.
- Get to know the Thriver Self and how it makes itself known.
- The facilitation of the Watcher visualization.

Group Share: Group participants share with one another whom they met during the live group visualization of the Watcher.

Group Support: Group participants listen and verbally and nonverbally support those who are sharing their Watcher visualization experiences.

Homework: Simply acknowledge in a few words how you feel about what you have read so far and have learned in the group. Use the prompts from the homework section in chapter 2.

Homework: Trace an early Invisible Loss memory in between Weeks 3 and 4. Use the exercise prompts from the homework section in chapter 2. Share in online forum and support each other's shares.

Week 4: Awareness Phase—Unlocking Your Story
Week 4 is about the first time that group participants unlock their Waiting Rooms and figure out how they got there to begin with.

Reading: Chapter 3: Unlocking Your Story

Objectives:

- Group members familiarize themselves with the template for Unlocking Your Invisible Loss.
- Understand the difference between Waiting Room life and a fully expressed Original Self life.

Group Share: Participants share memories of Original Self with one another.

Group Support: Group participants support one another when Moments of Impact are shared while in session by validating the shares.

Homework: Use the Unlock Your Waiting Room template and go through this exercise in between Weeks 4 and 5. Use the exercise prompts from the homework section in chapter 3. Share your discovery and the unlocking of your Waiting Room with the group.

Week 5: Defensiveness Phase—The Mental Stack
This week is about shedding the Survivor thoughts and attempting, for the first time, to take back the controls. The group participants will be learning how to stack for the first time, becoming attuned to what the Survivor thought patterns are. We will undertake this task here with this new practice of Mental Stacking.

Reading: Chapter 4: The Mental Stack—Cleanse, Pattern, Reframe

Objectives:

- Explain the purpose of the Daily Stack.
- Group facilitator to construct a 3-Tiered Mental Stack while in session as an example and to help participants create a daily routine of Mental Stacking for the first time.
- Group participants take a few minutes to write out their first Stack. Facilitator reviews their first Stacks and helps participants find Patterns or repetitions—emotions they expressed frequently.
- Ask the rest of the group to listen and support each participant during the sharing process.

Group Share: It is critical for the group to share their concerns, challenges, and difficulties as they start to familiarize themselves with Mental Stacking. By Week 6, group participants would greatly benefit from having completed seven daily 3-Tiered Mental Stacks.

Group Support: Share your Daily Stack in your online forum and support one another by commenting and validating other participants' Stacks.

Homework: Complete seven rounds of the 3-Tiered Mental Stacks.

Week 6: Action Phase—Escape from the Waiting Room with Plug-Ins
This week is about stepping into action after five weeks of discovering Invisible Losses, learning how to cleanse, pattern finding, and reframing. The group participants go from working on their thoughts with Mental Stacking to converting all those Reframes into action and taking their first step out of the Waiting Room.

Reading: Chapter 5: Escape from the Waiting Room

Objectives:

- It is fundamental for group participants to understand the difference between a 3-Tiered Mental Stack and a 4-Tiered Mental Stack and how to take action on a Plug-In.

- Group participants learn how to make a Plug-In timely, actionable, and achievable.

- Group participants focus on creating a Daily Stack routine.

Group Share: Group participants share examples of Plug-Ins with each other by utilizing all 4 tiers of the stack. They should share seven Daily Stacks with Plug-Ins between Weeks 6 and 7.

Group Support: Participants are encouraged to create a daily Plug-In derived from the Mental Stack. Each Plug-In helps to break the participants out of the Waiting Room. Sharing the daily Plug-Ins in the online forum is key during this week.

Homework: Complete seven rounds of the 4-Tiered Mental Stacks.

Week 7: Divergent Phase—The Fork in the Road
During this week, the group participants are starting to say yes to their Original Selves. This next phase feels rebellious, as the Survivor Self is being inhibited further with less questioning of the Watcher Self.

Reading: Chapter 6: The Fork in the Road

Objectives:

- Participants are encouraged to begin discovering the Thriver Self that is being reborn.

- The group facilitator guides participants to exploration and expression of the Thriver with discussions around newly reframed thoughts, ideas, hobbies, and activities.

- Participants create a narrative of their day from the perspective of the Watcher.

Group Support: Support one another during this week as the basic 4-Tiered Mental Stack is changing to an intermediate Mental Stack.

Group Share: Watcher Day exercise.

Homework: Seven daily intermediate Stacks: Watcher Cleanse.

Week 8: Integration Phase—Rediscovery of Original Self
Participants are encouraged to place the Thriver Self in charge of decisions and to add the wisdom of the Watcher Self. Integrating the selves brings forth the Original Self. The participants have exited the Waiting Room but may consciously choose to go back and rest or use the skills of Life Reentry to repeat the process as needed.

Reading: Chapter 7: Coming Home to Yourself

Objectives:

- Live guidance of the Thriver Bridge to the Past visualization. Help participants create their own definitions of joy, love, and adventure.

- Point out Thriver's voice in different shares throughout the group session, as well as lingering influences of the Survivor.

- Explain strategies, such as designing a new Thriver memory, that foster distance from the Survivor and reconnect with the Thriver.

- Explain the importance of maintaining recently introduced thinking patterns and habits through the Stacks. In other words, keep group members stacking, especially in this final phase.

Group Support: Help with validating newly remembered memories.

Group Share: Sharing the Thriver memory or memories deriving from the guided visualization exercise. Share other Thriver memories with one another.

Homework: Thriver Day. Write about your day from the perspective of the Thriver to find your Original Self at play.

Week 9: Integration Phase—Final Completion

Group participants set new goals and express new wishes for where they want to head next in their lives. This session focuses on completion of the participants' first Life Reentry journey and looking ahead to creating their mission statement. This is an exciting and rewarding week, as everyone has worked hard to get to this new beginning.

Reading: Chapter 8: Final Integration and Conclusion: You Have the Last Words

Objectives:

- Acknowledge and reward participants for their hard work.

- Explain and address potential setbacks when returning to a forward-looking perspective on life, and ask the group participants to plan a day of the Thriver, for example.

- Introduce them to the Conversation of Selves Stack while at the same time monitoring their progress, and help them plan their Waiting Room day when needed.

Group Support: Help with focusing on a daily maintenance routine, as they are about to transition to the Maintenance support group structure.

Group Share: Original Self-Inventory newly updated scores.

Homework: Write your mission statement.

Life Reentry Maintenance Support Group Structure: Coming Home to Yourself

Week 10 marks the end of the first Life Reentry cycle and the beginning of the Maintenance group structure. The group can now meet biweekly or weekly depending on its needs. Each session begins with the first thirty minutes dedicated to the group members sharing their weekly or biweekly Plug-Ins and focuses on Watcher and Thriver language use throughout the remainder of the meeting. Maintaining focus on interactions out of the Waiting Room is important during the group sessions. Survivor-based language is OK to be shared, but it is important to focus on reframing it.

Reading: Go back to the book whenever you feel like you need to revisit a section so you can maintain your Stacks.

Objectives: To maintain a daily practice of Stacks so that you keep reentering life without any long stays in the Waiting Room.

Group Support: Share any setbacks with each other, and reframe any Survivor thoughts that are emerging.

Group Share: Share how your last week went. What kind of Plug-Ins did you do that impacted your week?

Homework: Daily 4-Tiered Mental Stacks.

The healing and transformative power of the Life Reentry groups lies in the ability to articulate something we have been feeling but have never been able to find the words for; to cleanse these feelings in front of an audience who then validates these newly found emotions; and lastly to hold one another accountable with the Mental Stacks. Life Reentry then becomes easier to achieve in the longer term.

Additional Resources

Life Reentry Website: lifereentry.com

Invisible Loss Library: invisiblelosses.com

Christina Rasmussen Website: christinarasmussen.com

Glossary of Terms

Baseline Story: The "before" Life Reentry snapshot of an individual's perception of their past.

Cleanse: A stream-of-consciousness unfiltered and unedited writing of one's thoughts.

4-Tiered Mental Stack: The Cleanse: The transcription of automatic routinely based unconscious thoughts. Survivor Pattern: Subtracting the thoughts of fear and doubt. Watcher Reframe: Reframing fear and doubt. Plug-In: Translating the reframed thought into action.

Invisible Loss: A feeling that is more subtle than grief, yet a persistent emotion that is not easily defined due to a lack of societal validation. An Invisible Loss can be invisible to others but not to the Self or invisible to others as well as to the Self.

Life Reentry process: A mental health model for helping people "come back to life" after the initial aftermath of a devastating event.

Maintenance mode: Life Reentry is followed by a maintenance Stack practice. Regaining control over the Survivor Self requires a daily or weekly reset to avoid long-term Waiting Room stays.

Mental Stacking: A daily practice of stacking thoughts. The ability to manually layer one's thoughts, replacing unconscious Survivor-based thinking.

Moment of Impact: Some sort of rejection, either a verbal or nonverbal judgment that alters our early notion of self.

Original Self: The Self who we are in the absence of external influence.

Plug-In: A low-risk action step that will activate an exit from the Waiting Room.

Primary Invisible Loss: Some sort of rejection, either a verbal or nonverbal judgment that alters our early notion of self. An early and primary acute inner emotional response to an otherwise "normal" event. The loss of who we were prior to that Moment of Impact.

Survivor Self: A mindset that prioritizes survival over thriving. It occupies the past or the future. Never the present.

Survivor thought pattern: A repetitive fear- or doubt-based thought about the future.

3-Tiered Mental Stack: This daily Mental Stack has a Cleanse, a Survivor Pattern discovery, and a Watcher Reframe (see 4-Tiered Mental Stack, above).

Thriver Self: A mindset that prioritizes fun, adventure, and the present moment.

Waiting Room: A mindset of procrastination and life lived in waiting mode or in limbo.

Watcher Self: A mindset derived from the wisdom one accumulates over time, but it is often overshadowed by fear-based thoughts. It presents as a witness to life's significant moments.

Notes

Introduction

1 "Generalized Anxiety Disorder (GAD)," Anxiety and Depression Association of America (ADAA), October 25, 2022, adaa.org /understanding-anxiety/generalized-anxiety-disorder-gad.

Chapter 2: The Fragmented Self—Survivor, Watcher, Thriver

1 Christopher Nolan, *Inception: The Shooting Script* (San Raphael, CA: Insight Editions, 2010).

Chapter 4: The Mental Stack—Cleanse, Pattern, Reframe

1 Anne Craig, "Discovery of 'Thought Worms' Opens Window to the Mind," *Queen's University Gazette*, July 13, 2020, queensu.ca/gazette /stories/discovery-thought-worms-opens-window-mind.

Chapter 5: Escape from the Waiting Room

1 Rachel Aviv, "How Elizabeth Loftus Changed the Meaning of Memory," *New Yorker*, March 29, 2021, newyorker.com/magazine /2021/04/05/how-elizabeth-loftus-changed-the-meaning-of -memory.

Chapter 7: Coming Home to Yourself

1 Mary Oliver, "The Summer Day," The Library of Congress, accessed October 31, 2023, loc.gov/programs/poetry-and-literature/poet -laureate/poet-laureate-projects/poetry-180/all-poems/item/ poetry-180-133/the-summer-day/.

2 Robert Roy Britt, "Could Not Thinking at All Improve Your Memory?" *Medium*, July 1, 2019, elemental.medium.com/the-art -and-science-of-remembering-df393a17685b.

3 Trevor English, "How Do We . . . What Was It . . . Remember Things?," November 17, 2019, *Interesting Engineering*, interestingengineering .com/science/how-do-we-what-was-it-remember-things.

Appendix: Support Group Guide

1 Elisabeth Kübler-Ross, *On Death and Dying: What the Dying Have to Teach Doctors, Nurses, Clergy and Their Own Families* (New York: Scribner, 2019).

About the Author

Christina Rasmussen is an acclaimed grief educator and best-selling author of *Second Firsts* (Hay House, 2013) and *Where Did You Go?* (Harper One, 2018). In 2010, four years after her thirty-five-year-old spouse passed away from Stage 4 colon cancer, she created the Life Reentry process, which launched her on a mission to bring compassion, grace, and validation to thousands while simultaneously establishing an exit from what she termed the *Waiting Room*. Christina holds a master's degree in guidance and counseling (University of Durham). She is currently finishing her master of fine arts degree in painting and drawing (Academy of Art University). Her grief work has been featured on ABC News and in *Women's World*, the *Washington Post*, and the White House Blog. In her spare time, she is learning to play the piano and planning her first trip to the edge of space. She works and lives in Austin, Texas, with her husband, Eric, and their two dogs.